Custom Motorcycle Fabrication

Timothy Remus

Published by:
Wolfgang Publications Inc.
P.O. Box 223
Stillwater, MN 55082
www.wolfpub.com

Legals

First published in 2014 by Wolfgang Publications Inc.,
P.O. Box 223, Stillwater MN 55082

ISBN 13: 978-1-935828-79-2

Printed and bound in U.S.A.

Custom Motorcycle Fabrication

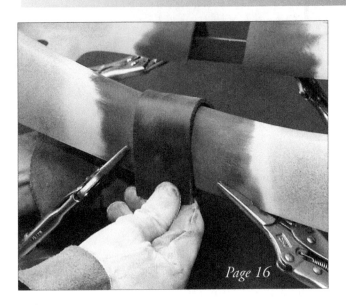

Page 16

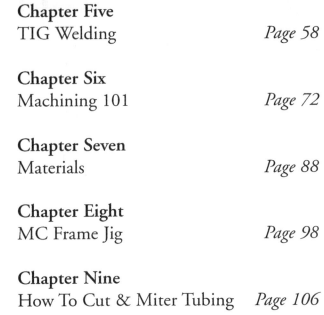

Page 110

Page 67

Acknowledgements

This is about my eighty third motorcycle-building book. And near the end of each one there comes the time for the thank-yous.

For this book I enlisted the help of three outside authors and a lot of my mechanically inclined friends.

The outside authors include: Steve "Brewdude" Garn and Paul Wideman, both well-known writers and fabricators (and shop owners). The third outside author is Deb Shade, great photographer and writer, well known in the Minneapolis/St. Paul motorhead community. To all three, thanks for the help, for working under tight deadlines, and doing it all for something less than a king's ransom.

The list of mechanically inclined friends who helped on this one is as long as my arm. Which makes me realize how lucky I am to have them as friends.

In no particular order, here they are:

Donnie Smith and his ace fabricator and welder, Rob Roehl. The brothers Shadley, Paul and Mark, and all the members of their very diverse and helpful crew. Kurt Senescal and Pat Kary at Creative Metalworks, a hidden gem of a Minneapolis shop.

Not only do all these welders, fabricators, mechanics an helpers let me into their shop, put with my camera, and help write captions; their skill, attention to detail, and dedication to their crafts always inspire me to be the best I can at everything I do, from photography to working on old rusty hot rods.

Introduction

Merriam-Webster defines the word custom, when used to modify a word like motorcycle, as: *made to fit the needs or requirements of a particular person.*

That custom motorcycle you build will indeed need to fit you ergonomically, but more important, mentally. A custom bike is an expression of your soul, of what's deep inside your head. A statement about what's really important in your life.

It might be really hauling ass down a curvy road that gets your rocks off. Or it might just be the simple pleasure of riding your own very bare-bones bike equipped with only the essentials - two wheels, one gas tank, one oil tank, one motor, tranny and primary drive, and the other necessities like a seat, bars and minimal lights and electronics.

Whether you're building a Cafe Racer, or a Chopper, there's one more important word in this whole custom motorcycle thing, and word is - *build.* As in, build the bike, or at least most of the bike, yourself. If it's going to be a truly unique motorcycle, some of the parts need to be unique as well. They need to be *fabricated,* either from scratch, or by making creative use of something else, something that might not have been meant for use on a motorcycle at all.

The intent of this book is to show two things: One, the specific skills and methods that are used and needed if you are going to fabricate a set of bars, or modify a frame. Two, we've tried to illuminate the whole process of building a custom bike. Even in the case of a simple bike, it's a lot of damned work. There are a few chapters in this book that follow the building of a bike from the first sketch on a napkin to the finished and roaring machine. We've tried to show not just how much work it is, but the numerous decisions that need to be made along the way. And how, ever with a good plan, the project may change along the way.

You can't build a set of pipes unless you know how to weld. And you can't make your own axle spacers out of brass unless you know how to run a lathe or mill. Unless you're a pro, it's likely that your skill set doesn't include all the skills needed to build this new bike. But one thing is for sure, when you're done with the build, you will have more than a new motorcycle. You will have at least one brand new skill.

For some, the act of building the machine is ultimately just as satisfying as riding it down the road. And I don't think there are any of us who don't derive a lot of pleasure from making something unique, useful, and beautiful in some way or other, with our own hands.

So have at it. Dream. Plan. Act.

Chapter One

A Shadley Built Bagger

Built to Ride!

Some custom bikes are built for show, and some are built for go. In the case of this long, lean Bagger from the Shadley Brothers, it's a little of both. Bob Garone is a friend of the Shadleys, and a good customer. When he told Mark he needed a Bagger, Mark decided it should be a Bagger in

name only. This very one-off machine shares very little DNA with the Baggers that roll off the line in Milwaukee.

It was during the ride to Sturgis from California with friends that Mark arranged to buy the last of Arlen Ness' rubber mount five-speed

Though the 120R engine wears the bar and shield logo, the rest of this Bagger is from the Aftermarket Company starting with the Arlen Ness frame, Paul Yaffe Lights, Baker tranny gears, Sinister fairing and Shadley Bros one-off fabrications.
Photo credit: Dino Petrocelli

frames from the King himself. For the go part of the equation, Mark bought a 120 SE Twin Cam engine from Harley-Davidson, mated it up to a six-speed transmission case filled with Baker gears.

The long stretched theme starts with the Arlen Ness frame, which came with five inches of stretch in the top tube. Bolted to that frame is a late model Harley-Davidson front fork assembly that pivots on a pair of triple trees with five degrees of rake. At the back of the bike Mark used a 2002-and-up swingarm with the one-inch axle, stretched an additional inch and a half.

To skinny up the "sheet metal" a Sinister single-headlight outer fairing was mated to a modified Road Glide inner fairing. If the rear bags somehow don't look just exactly like a stock Harley bags, it's because the crew sectioned the bags two inches, which turned out to be one of the toughest single tasks they tackled during the build due to the shape of the stock bags.

The rear fender with the integral "bag fillers" and taillight/blinker lights is likewise a very unique piece made from a Klock Werks Softail fender, a set of Yaffe LED lights and a number of fabricated parts.

Some bikes just plain got it going on, and this is a prime example. A bike you can enter in the bike show, ride two up at highly illegal speeds, or - if you've really got the stones - take to Bonneville to see exactly what she's got.

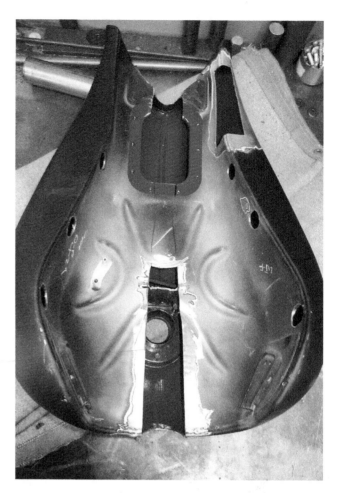

A Victory gas tank came in for some serious mods before it could be adapted to the Ness frame - like finding a way to install the fuel pump assembly...

The foundation of this Bagger is a five-inch-stretch Arlen Ness, FXR-style five-speed frame.

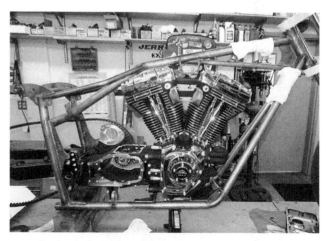

Hauling ass down the highway requires abundant power, supplied in this case by a 120R engine from Harley-Davidson. H-D tranny case will house a Baker 6-speed gearset.

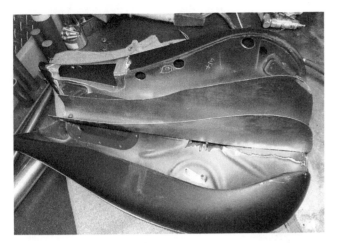

... and add a tunnel...

...and will be mated up with this factory Road Glide inner fairing, with the radio receiver area made into gauge pockets.

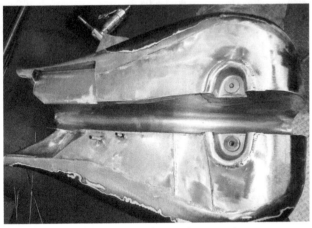

... and a new bottom as shown here with a cut out for the rocker box.

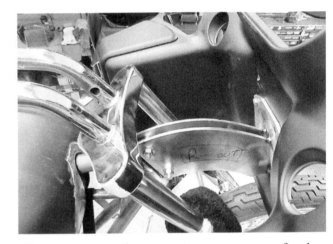

Here you can see the raw main upper mount for the fairing assembly.

A fairing yes, but not just another factory unit. This outer fairing is from Sinister...

A little farther along, the mount looks to be a much more finished piece.

The frame came in for a lot of modification at the back - this heavy duty battery box will become an integral part of the frame.

... here are the new struts tack-welded in place. The lower mount was moved back an equal amount through the use of a stretched 2002-and-up Bagger swingarm...

Once the box is welded in place it will serve to strengthen the back of the frame. Some braces under the tranny were eliminated as well in order to leave space for the oil bag.

... with a lower shock mount that was relocated to the very end of the 'arm, as seen in this progress shot.

Getting the shock to line up with the concave cutout in the saddle bags required moving the upper shock mount back with longer struts as shown...

Hand-fabricated side covers hide the battery box and some of the electronics.

9

Here's the left side cover clamped in place prior to welding.

Deciding where to put the bag mounts and support took a lot of trial fitting - rear bag-mount location was determined first, which then set the location of the front mount.

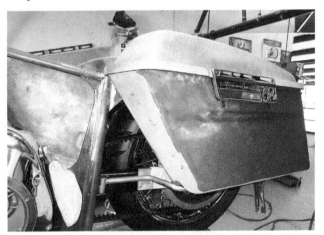

The lower supports for the bags are factory units modified to fit this new frame.

The strut for the fender and bag-mounts - mocked up here - is made from 3/4 inch aluminum stock, bolted to the new shock strut.

You can see one stock bag and one in the process of being stretched and narrowed.

Narrowing and stretching the bags took a lot of time, note the section Russ removed to skinny-up the bag. Stretching required the addition of material from another set of bags.

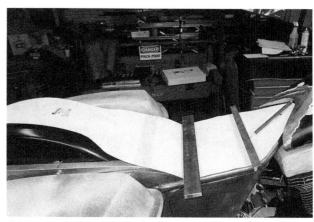

Time to decide where the bends and curves need to be.

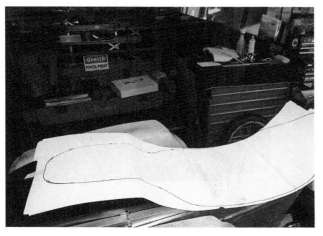

Seat pan starts out as an outline drawn on a piece of light board.

Simple bends are done on the sheet metal brake...

The outline is then transferred to a piece of sheet metal and cut out as shown.

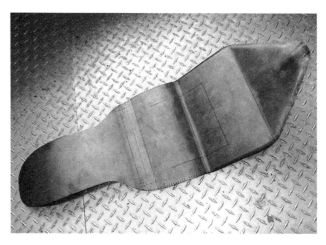

Curved tail section is shaped by hand.

Mock up shot shows skinny bags and rear fender, gas tank and seat pan, all bolted in place.

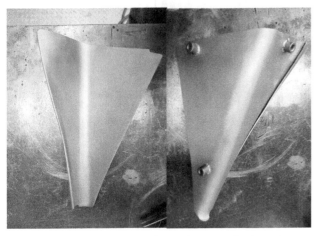

These concave filler panels are bent up by hand - once the shape is correct the threaded bungs are added.

Early shot shows the bags mounted, before...

The filler panels help the bags blend with, and become an integral part of the bike.

...the filler panels are fabricated and bolted in place.

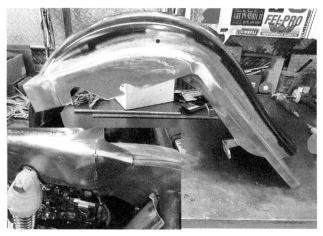

After fabrication from sheet stock the panels are welded to the fender...

A long list of modifications were made to both the inner and outer fairing starting with...

Next it's time for a test fit.

...the addition of the speedo/tach cluster where the radio was originally placed. The housing isn't a perfect fit, and requires the addition of crescents...

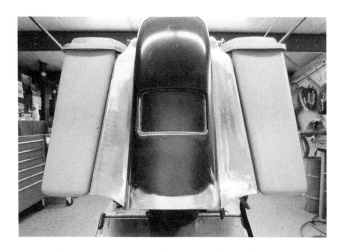

... and some trimming of the panels so they merge nicely with the fender.

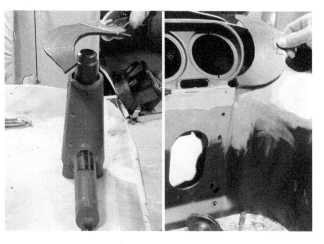

...the crescents are cut from scrap plastic, the heat gun is used to make them easy to shape before...

...they are glued into place on either side of the gauge cluster. Note how one small-gauge location has been eliminated on each side.

... but Russ and Mark decided it would look much better with a 5 inch beam, which meant filling in the front section...

The original Sinister outer fairing came with a bolt-on windshield, which the boys modified slightly and glued in place to eliminate the seam.

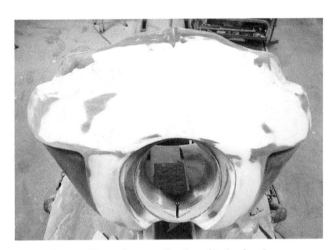

... and installing the smaller headlight bucket.

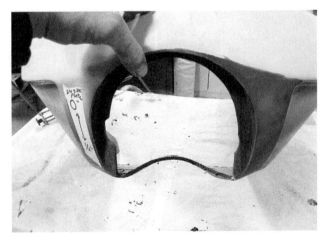

The original fairing was designed to use a 7 inch headlight...

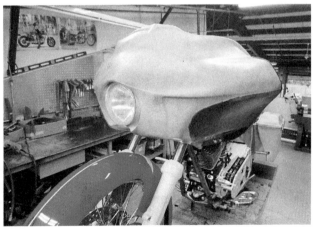

The new fairing, complete with 5 inch headlight, almost ready for paint.

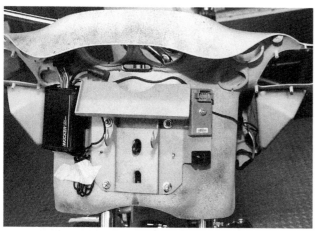

To keep everything nice and neat, the crew added brackets for the electrical modules and components to the backside of the inner fairing.

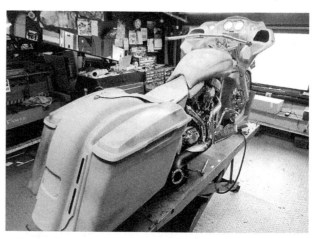

Almost ready for paint, you get an idea how long and lean this high speed cruiser really is.

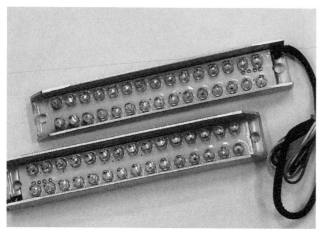

LED lights from Paul Yaffe are used at the rear of the bike.

A BDL belt drive connects the 120 inch engine and 6-speed transmission.

A Badlands module made it easy to use the two light assemblies to be used for tail, brake and turn-lights.

Front fender from RWD wraps the spoked 21 inch front wheel. Front end is late model unit from H-D, with lower legs (shaped by S.B.), rotors and calipers from PM.

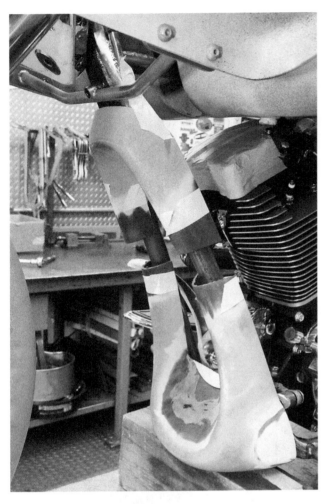

Mark deemed the air dam too short, here you see the first mock-up of the stretched air dam.

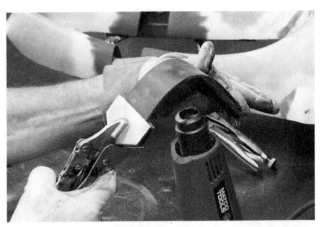

Stretching the air dam is done with material borrowed from a set of bags (made from the same plastic) made soft and pliable with the heat gun again.

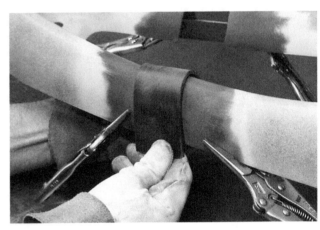

First a test fit. Once the shape is right, it's locked in by cooling the plastic. Next comes the trimming...

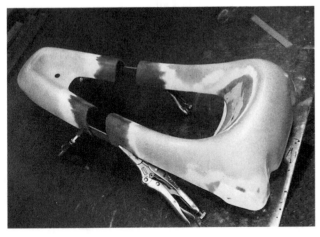

Steel straps and a group of vise grips are used to pre-assemble the air dam on the bench.

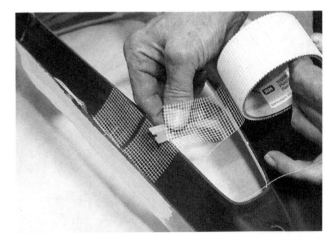

... before the plugs are glued in place and reinforced with webbing from the hardware store meant to reinforce sheet-rock seams.

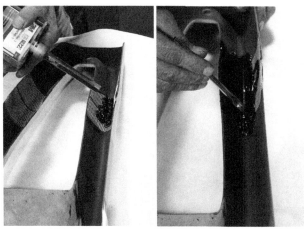

Now another coat of the two-part material is added to strengthen the air dam from the inside - 3M 08223. Watch out, it sets up fast.

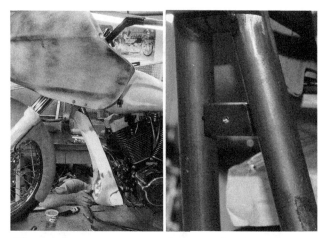

The upper mount is a simple piece of mild steel, drilled and tapped and welded in place between the two downtubes.

Russ likes to finish with 2-part plastic spot putty, "I know it's going to adhere to the plastic and it's easy to sand. The air dam needs to be washed thoroughly and scuffed first so the putty will stick."

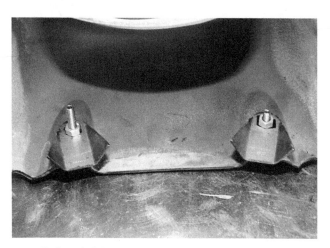

Small, hand-fabricated brackets for the bottom of the air dam will be welded to the frame...

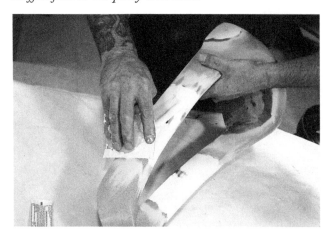

Most of the initial finishing of the spot putty is done by hand with 80 grit paper.

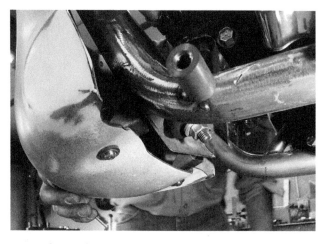

... as shown here.

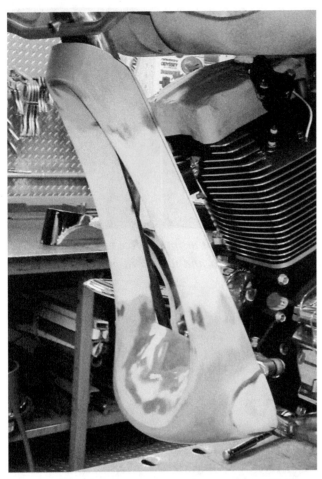

Air dam stretched and mounted to chassis - the final check before disassembly and paint.

Another final check outside to check fitment of gauges and warning lights.

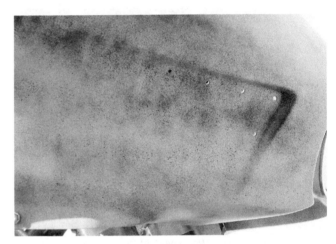

Holes in the fairing are drilled for mini LED turn signals.

All fabrication is complete, it's a good idea to roll the bike outside to check the final lines - and get some good photos.

The bare chassis ready for sand blasting.

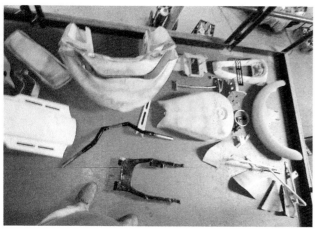

In the middle of priming and body work on a total of 48 separate parts.

First batch of miscellaneous parts in the paint booth.

You can see the floor board/brake pedal mounting stanchions.

The fairing and other parts primed and ready for paint.

After body work, a check on fitment of rear the panels and fender fitment.

Like all the parts, the first color to go on the fairing is this light blue basecoat.

Frame molded and painted with basecoat.

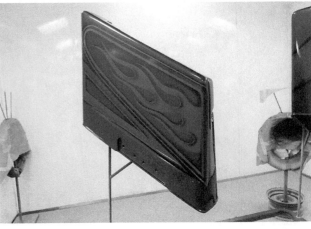

Finally they spray the whole thing with more of the candy cobalt - the cobalt gets deeper and darker, and the flames become more muted.

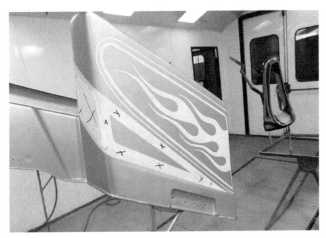

After basecoat, the parts get a coat of clear, then a wet sanding, followed by the graphic masks.

Next they shoot the bag with candy cobalt blue from H of K, pull the graphic tape or mask, and then shadow the flames and the graphic.

Same thing happens to the tank, which is shown here painted with the basecoat.

After applying clear, and sanding, John Hartnett applies the flame mask.

The fairing ready for the first coat of cobalt. All the parts go through the same multi-step painting process...

The pattern repeats. Spray the tank with cobalt blue, pull the mask, shade the flames with an airbrush, then more cobalt blue.

...you can see how much work it to do the layouts and painting of all the parts.

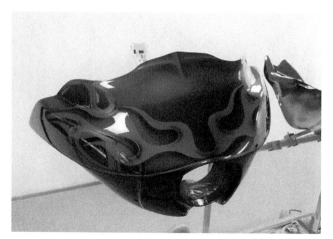

After the final coats of cobalt, the outer fairing and all the other parts get multiple coats of clear with sanding between coats...

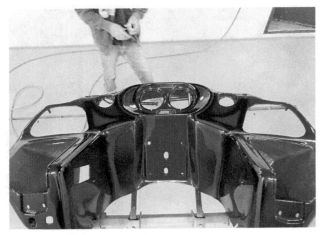

...to create an incredible and durable shine.

Here's the early stage of assembly with the swingarm and tranny in place...

The new 120R Harley motor was disassembled completely, powdercoated, striped and polished, and then reassembled.

...next the short block goes in...

After the polishing and/or painting parts like this tranny case, all the threads are chased with a tap to clean out any paint or compound in the threads.

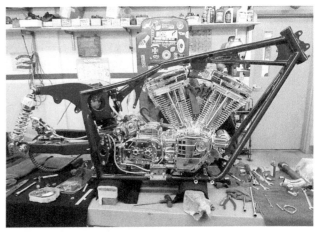

...followed by the heads and cylinders.

Front end is now installed, along with the belt drive, and the coil assemblies.

Inner fairing is almost finished...

The assembly takes time and patience. The rear fender and struts are in place. Also the rear lights and wiring to the back of the bike is done.

...close up shows the Tach and speedo, mounted where the radio used to be.

Finally up on two wheels, bag supports are in place - it's starting to look like a motorcycle.

Left side shot shows the various components mounted to the inner fairing.

Almost done, but a lot left to do. The wiring harness is fabricated in the shop, wire by wire.

Off the hoist finally, Note how the narrowed bags skinny-up the whole rear of the bike.

DYNO TIME.

We like to run all newly assembled bikes on the dyno. First we just run the bike along at a easy pace for about 10 minuets Then we shut it down, let it cool and go over the bike fore any leaks, lose bolts, anything that may be a problem. It could be a lose drive belt, a brake rotor heating up, or a small fuel leak. We also check the fuel mixture on that first run at cruise speed. If it's got a carb and needs a change, we shut it off and make a jet change. With an injected bike we do the tune when it's on the run. After everything looks good and any needed adjustments are made we run it for about 30 minutes at a slow cruise speed. We vary the speed, but still go very easy. Then we do the same thing we did the first time. Let it rest. And go over the whole set-up again. The bike never gets W.O.T. or even close at this point. Its just a controlled, easy, brake-in.

If the weather is conducive we take the bike out on the road. The nice thing about the dyno is, if the weather is bad we can run a bike as much as we like. Here in the Northeast, even in the winter we look for a warmer day because there is no heat in the dyno room and it gets very cold. But if we are heading to a rally and need to have the bike ready we will run it for as much as 2 to 3 hours and then do an oil change, so the bike has had a little time to seat in before it gets into rally traffic or the owner gives it a blast. Either way it's a safe way to run in a new engine or new combo, the way we do it just makes sense. WE DON'T DO FULL POWER PULLS ON NEW MOTORS.

The combination of a stretched frame, and single headlight fairing, give this Bagger a svelte profile that belies its true size.

The rear view provides more of the same; narrowed bags, victory tank and John's long flowing flames all work to reinforce the stretched and ready-to-run profile.

Captions by Mark Shadley and the Shadley Crew

Chapter Two

Billy's Shovel-Glide

Swap Meet Shovel Glide - and a Whole Lot More

The Shadley Brothers from Whitman, Massachusetts are well known as builders of some very nice and very fast custom bikes. The boys like to ride, thus the bikes they build - no matter how expensive or elaborate - are built to run.

They can also be (somewhat) thrifty, as illustrated by this bike that came to be known as Billy's Shovel-Glide. If you ask Billy about the genesis of the Shovel-Glide, he explains that it started out as just an older Shovel that needed

Billy's ride isn't a bike you see everyday. Definitely a Shovel, yet one with some nice modern touches - like a complete late-model front end, Dyna bags, disc brake in the rear and Road Glide fairing. Plus a great paint job and completely rebuilt engine and transmission.

some love. "I bought it four years ago," explains Billy. "The owner passed away, and his son sold me the bike. It was in pretty good condition, a fairly stock 1979 Low Rider. I ran it around for two months then I quit riding it."

"My plan at that point was to make a ground pounder out of it... but I never really got too far. A couple of years later Mark Shadley took a look at the bike and talked me out of my plan. It was Mark who suggested we make a Bagger out of it."

"When Mark explained what be wanted to do with the bike I told him we should keep it to a budget, that I didn't want to spend way more on the bike than it's worth. The bike actually sat in the Shadley shop for awhile before we started to work on it. And that gave us time to collect parts from a number of swap meets."

"In fact, most of the parts we used to upgrade and build this bike came from swap meets: The Road Glide fairing, the late model Harley-Davidson front end, the wheels, the flat-sided tanks, the rear brake caliper, late-model hand controls, all the switches, lights and directionals, and even the Dyna saddle bags, all those parts are parts we found at swap meets - at a fraction of the cost of new components. What we did buy new was things like the internal parts we needed to completely rebuild the engine, and the transmission."

Mark Shadley explains that though the intent was to build a unique budget Bagger they fell short on the budget part. "What started out to be a modest build turned into a full-on project. There was a lot of fab time: mounting bags, gas tanks, and fairing. It's all late-model sheet metal, we had to fit a dash, get new engine cases, and do a complete engine overhaul, install a new gear set and do a total electrical rebuild including the charging circuit, ignition and re-wiring all the modules."

"Just before we started on this Billy had a pretty bad accident on a Road King and spent four months in the hospital - thus the bloody Billy nick name. When that happened I decided that maybe what he really needed was a rider, not a bar hopper rigid."

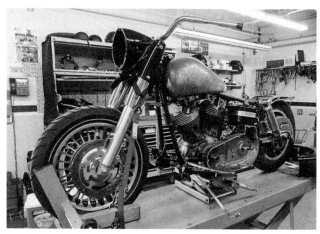

Not a thing of beauty, at least not yet...

... the Shovelhead engine and frame date to 1978,

Front and rear wheels are 2007 and up H-D. Gas tanks are flat-side style.

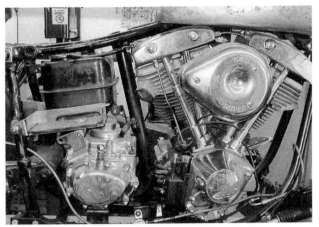

The stock Shovel is scheduled for a complete rebuild by Mark Shadley, with mostly S&S components, including new cases and oil pump.

Mock-up session… "what if we bolted on a Road Glide fairing, and used stock FLH front and rear fenders? Hey, it doesn't look too bad…

The front end is later 2012 unit from H-D. The Road King nacelle didn't work out and the fairing was added instead.

…and then we could bolt on those Dyna Switchback bags we bought at the swap meet - after fabricating mounts for the bags…

Gas tanks are later flat-side designs, along with a soon-to-come aftermarket dash. Installing the tanks meant installation of new mounts as well.

…damn, looks like a motorcycle."

Why buy new when slightly used will do? Dash from Milwaukee Iron is a swap meet find, here Leo does a test fit.

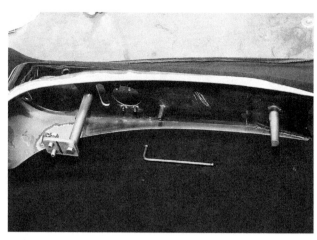

The two brackets are bolted to the dash...

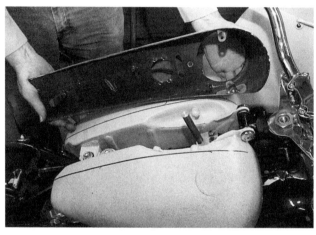

The plan is to mount the dash with two fabricated brackets...

... then another test fit - which shows all is well except the way the dash fails to follow the tank's contour at the very back.

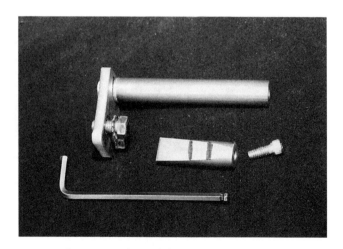

... seen here. Simple and functional, anyone can make something like this.

A series of slots, done with a small powered hacksaw, make it possible to bend the tail end of the dash so it follows the shape of the tank.

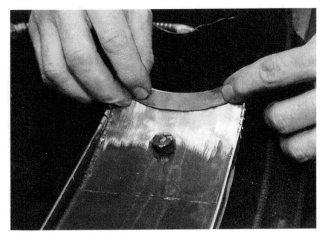

Once the contour is established, a small piece of sheet metal is cut out and welding in place...

Early mock-up shot shows the beginning of an upper fairing bracket.

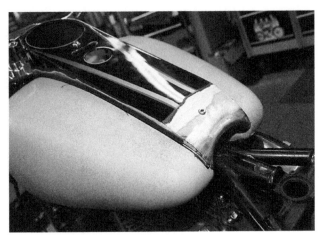

... to finish the dash and made a nice smooth concave surface that...

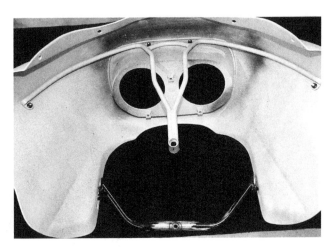

In this later shot you can see how the crew fabricated a finished upper and lower bracket...

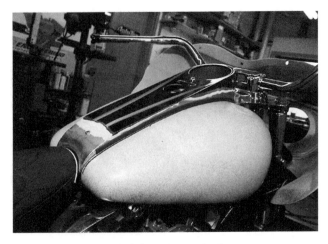

... meets the front of the seat perfectly.

... and how the lower bracket bolts to the horizontal strap that runs between the two downtubes, while the upper mount bolts to the bung welded to the neck.

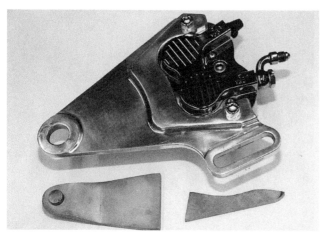

1) More swap meet scrounging. One JayBrake four-piston caliper and mount that needs just a little help in the bracket department to fit perfectly on the old Shovel.

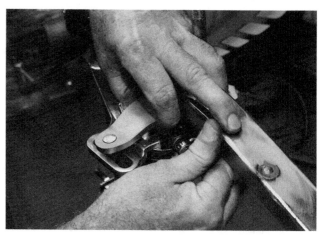

2) Here's the test fit of the bracket and pin that prevents the caliper from rotating when the brakes are applied.

3) Mark cuts a taper in the bracket...

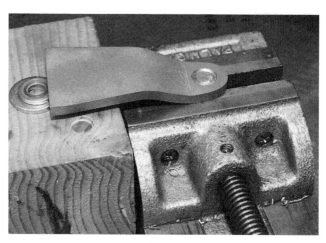

4) ...the taper matches the taper on the brake bracket stop pin as shown, both will make for a better weld...

5) ...the tapers leave room for a weld with better penetration.

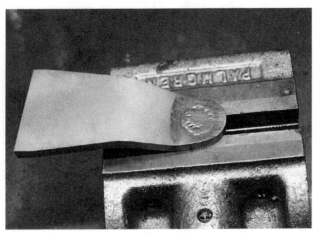

The finished weld has good penetration and is almost flush with the surface of the bracket.

Here's the swingarm and bracket after the final welding is completed. The swingarm will be polished and re-chromed before final assembly.

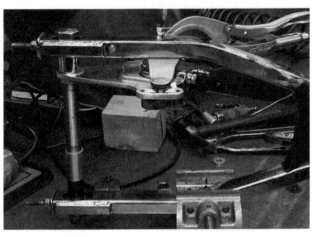

Next, the bracket is clamped to the swingarm - with the caliper in place to ensure the bracket is located correctly.

Time to reassemble the back of the bike, and check alignment of the caliper, and the rotor-to-caliper clearance...

Tack-welds are first, done so the bracket won't pull from the desired position during the final welding.

...complete with the rear fender, and the struts with the pins necessary for the mounting of the Dyna Switchback bags.

The Dyna bags are another swap meet find, they will work nicely on the Shovel as they're a bit smaller than Bagger bags and line up with the shock absorbers.

The fender's been reinforced as you can see here, to handle the vibration and the weight of the bags.

The brackets however, with their nice quick detach feature, had to be purchased from H-D.

With the help of a fabricated bracket, the rear-most bagger mount is attached to the fender strut. Some extra holes in the strut are filled at the same time.

The rear fender is a late model Bagger fender. The struts had to be moved out because this fender is 1/2 inch wider than the stock fender.

The bags are a close match with the originals - but offer better mounting and weather-proof latches.

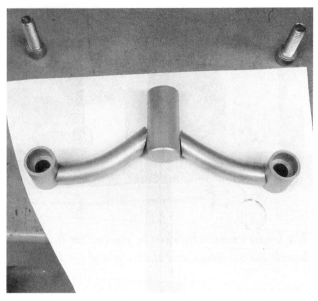

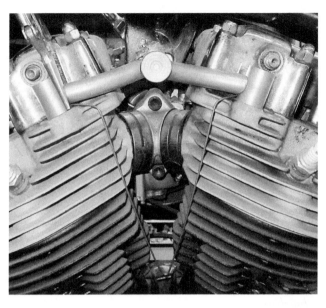

The fabrication of the Mark-Shadley-designed top engine mount starts with three bungs and two curved pieces of mild steel rod.

Here, you can see the start of the mount assembly set in place.

Next, weld the two long spears together...

... then clamp them in place...

... and weld them to the upper cross piece

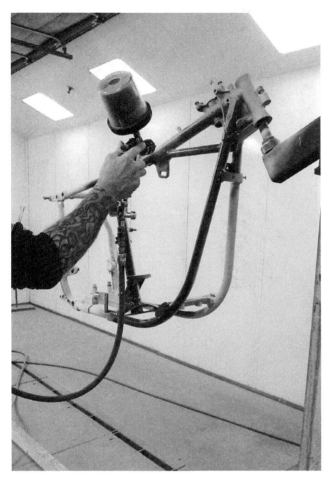

Painting starts with the frame. First comes sandblasting, then all welds are ground smooth. Next comes primer, wet sanding, sealer and finally it's ready for Russ to apply the final paint.

All of the sheet metal and body pieces ares prepped, primed and painted with PPG sealer followed by two coats of silva star, and multiple coats of PPG clear.

John Hartnett is the artist responsible for the design and the layout of the flames that flow across the fairing...

The same black urethane is used to clean up the appearance of the cast iron cylinders. Before painting, all casting flash and rough edges are removed.

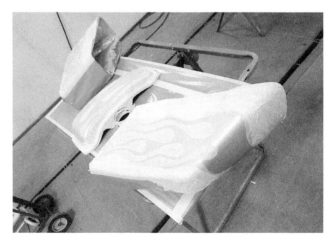

...as well as the saddle bags.

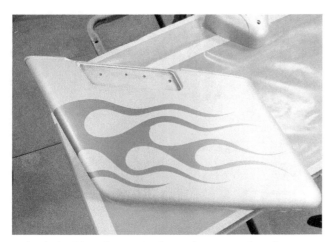

The light blue flames look good against the silver background.

Not exactly traditional flames in color or design...

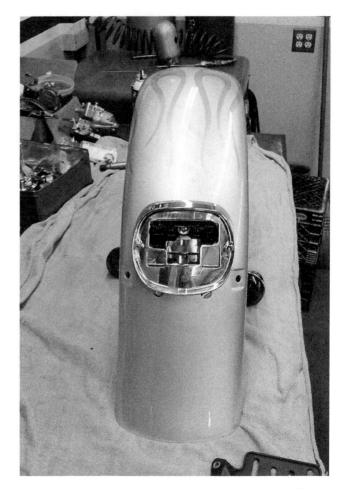

More swap meet goodies, a late model H-D taillight assembly.

... but John's stretched flames will give the bike a nice sense of motion.

As Mark explains, "On the tear down we found a crack in the cam bearing area, and the oil pump had sucked up some shit, so cases and pump are new. We kept the flywheels and rods, bored it .020 over and used Wiseco hi-comp pistons. Cam is a B+ from Andrews, with matching springs, carb is a Super E."

Assembly continues, front and rear suspension in place, no transmission yet.

Left side of final assembly. It's very important that all hardware is properly fitted and the right length, especially any hardware that can protrude inside the rear fender and contact the tire.

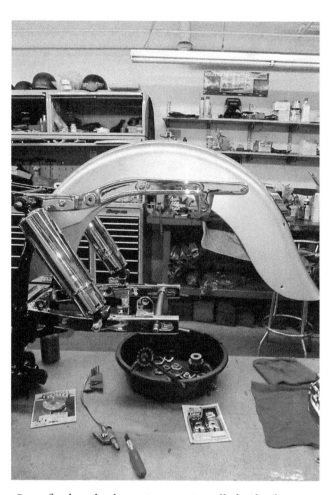

Rear fender, shocks, swingarm installed. Shocks are from Progressive. Swingarm bearings were changed, along with the seals.

You can see the 2010 style brakes, wheel and slider assembly. Custom mounts were needed to mount the cow bells to the lower trees.

The H-D four-speed tranny with new gears connects to the engine with a stock-style chain and clutch ass'm, though individual components are from Barnett and Jammer

The Road Glide light and blinker assembly looks right at home here. Curved license plate bracket is from Kuryakyn.

The Shovel-Glide is starting to look like a finished motorcycle...

....complete with the new Dyna bags, which line up nicely with the fender and the rear shocks.

It's an inside joke, a reference to Billy's accident on the Road King.

Shovel-Glide has a unique look, and nice lines thanks to the short windshield and the stretched flames.

A left front shot with fairing in place, along with the complete front end, and all wiring and cables.

Rear 3/4 view shows the Shovel-Glide minus only headlights and a few additional details.

Billy's new ride is a nice mix of old and new.

When asked, Billy described himself as "one very happy guy."

Though it certainly took more work - and money - that was originally planned, it's hard to complain when you look at the final outcome.

Q&A: Mark Shadley

Mark, have you always been involved in custom and high performance motorcycles?

It started at a very young age with dirt bikes and mini bikes.

Give us a little background on you and how you learned your fabrication and design skills?

At 13 I began work in an auto shop that did welding and rod repairs. So I learned welding and some metal fabrication. At 17 I started building custom parts for my bikes, in the early 1970's there weren't many parts available.

Give us a little background on the various businesses that you and your brother Paul own and run there in Whitman, MA. How big a part of the business is the custom bike business?

Our business, Shadley Bros/Auto Tec has four different divisions: Auto Repair, Auto Body, A motorcycle side which services any American made V-Twin and includes a retail parts store. We also tow for four local towns. The motorcycle side is a very important part, responsible for approximately 30% of the total business.

Including personal bikes, how many custom bikes do you build in a typical year

I would say around four to six custom bikes a year. Plus we handle many mild-custom jobs on a daily basis, i.e. bags, pipes, motor hop-up and paint.

What are the characteristics of a Shadley bike, the things that separate that machine from other custom machines. What are the one or two things that you strive for when building a new custom?

We work hard to build bikes that can be ridden, we focus attention on small details, and we build bikes that look like all the parts fit together. We strive to make sure there are no loose ends.

In terms of fabrication, what are the skills that a beginning bike builder needs to master?

Welding, preferably Heliarc. MIG is okay, but kind of rough for custom bikes. Also your hardware choices are crucial in order to keep the bike from falling apart.

And what are the tools you really need for a small motorcycle fabrication shop?

Everything you can get your hands on. A welder, belt sander, bandsaw, they're all important tools for fabrication work. But you can always build up as you go along and your skills will improve. You will eventually need more equipment, machine shop equipment, and it's handy to have metal shaping tools.

What are the mistakes that beginning builders make when building a complete custom motorcycle?

Don't build way over your head. Start with easier projects you can complete. As your skills improve, then take on more complicated jobs.

What is the one bit of wisdom you've learned during years of building bikes that you would pass along to a young builder - someone like you son Dean perhaps?

Think of what you want the bike to be, before you begin your task, do some homework, that way in the end you will have what you are looking to accomplish. Think before you start! And there is no incorrect in creating custom motorcycles, it's what you like. Don't be afraid to try out your ideas. Have fun, try new things and look at what others have done for ideas. Talk to those who have made it happen, most of them will help you.

Chapter Three

Dan's Dyna

A Rockin' Dyna from Donnie Smith Custom Cycles

When Dan Roche sat down with long-time friend Donnie Smith to discuss a new bike, his goals were pretty straightforward. First, because he wanted a bike that would make a good cruiser, he chose to start with a new 2013 Dyna Switchback, the Dyna that comes with a set of saddle bags and a windshield, both of which are easily detached.

Dan explained that he wanted to leave the bags and windshield option intact, but give the bike a bit more attitude. Some extra stretch and rake perhaps, and new sheet metal with nice paint. In the end though, Dan wanted something short of a

A Dyna with a difference. Dan Roche wanted something he could ride all day in comfort, with unique good looks and plenty of power - a bike with attitude, but one that still retained the H-D VIN number. A mild custom, mild enough that the cops and powers that be just let it roll by without a second look.

full-custom ride. Dan you see lives in Winnipeg, and though he spends a lot of time in the 'States, his bikes have to be mild enough that the cops and licensing authorities leave him alone and don't give him any trouble if he gets pulled over or needs new plates.

Once delivered to the shop, Donnie and Rob Roehl, Donnie's fabrication wizard, took a hard look at one of Harley's latest models. Their plan included a series of changes designed to give the bike that certain flow without going too far. To get the front wheel out there just a little, Rob pulled off the fork assembly and the tank, and did a rake and stretch job. Two inches of stretch and four additional degrees of rake seemed about right, combined with a set of five degree trees to prevent the trail figure from getting too far out of hand.

Sheet metal changes include the longer tank. Which is actually the stock tank moved forward an inch and a half, with a new tail added on the other end. Because the new bikes are getting more and more complex, Donnie and Rob decided to leave as much of the original wiring intact, including the fuel injection pump assembly located in the gas tank. They also left the regulator in its stock location, though now it's hidden inside the new air dam.

Like the gas tank, the side covers are fabbed and designed to leave the wiring and underlying structure in place. A new seat meant a new seat pan, one designed to be easily lifted on and off for access to the wiring. The rear fender follows the same theme, it's mostly pure stock Dyna, except for the Sportster taillight protected by Rob's small hood, and the license plate pad.

Additional visual treats include the one-off PMFR 23 inch front wheel, which just happens to match the rear Harley wheel, wrapped in an aftermarket fender from Hawg Halters. Dan's subdued paint job includes some black, done to tie the sheet metal in with the frame, which retains its stock black color.

There was just one more thing Dan wanted for this new ride. He wanted it to be fast. So when the finished bike came home, he immediately ripped it apart again, and installed a new 120R Twin Cam engine from Harley-Davidson.

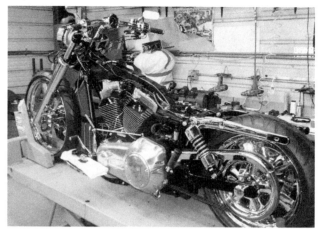

The bike started out as a stock 2013 Dyna Switchback. Here's the initial teardown.

The rake and stretch are so well done it looks like a stock frame - Rob stretched the frame 2 inches and increased the rake from 28 to 32 degrees. 5 degree trees help to bring the trail back to stock dimension.

One other change Dan wanted, was a bit more speed. Once home, he pulled this stock motor and installed a 120R from H-D.

If you look closely, you will see the fork tube extensions from Hawg Halters.

Stock battery box and electronics. One of the goals was to leave the stock electronics intact.

Another look at the neck area without paint - hard to tell from stock - and that was the whole idea.

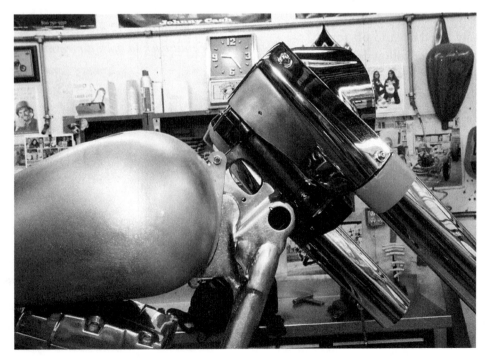

With the frame raked and new trees installed, it's a good idea to swing the fork both ways to make sure it clears the tank.

Progress shot shows the bike with the modified fender, new seat pan and stretched tank.

Rear fender is stock, with the addition of a custom hood and fabricated licensed plate mount. Note the round rod added to the fender edge, both for strength and to finish the edge.

The Dyna tank was moved forward 1-1/2 inches and stretched 4 inches in the back. Stock fuel injection pump assembly still fits in standard location.

Custom seat pan was fabricated from mild steel. Mounting pins locate the pan to the frame, and strips of Velcro hold it down. The idea was to keep the electronics under the seat as accessible as possible.

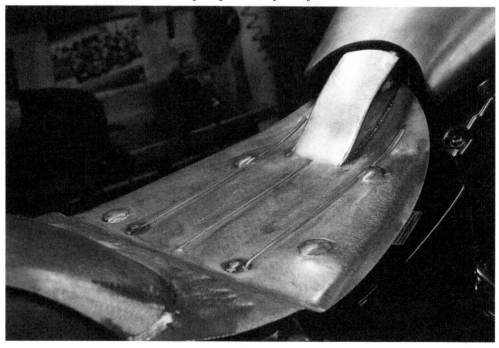

Cindy's Softail

Cindy's 2013 Softail in the Donnie Smith shop, being fitted with a set of Ballistic bags and fender. Bag mounts are from Cycle Vision.

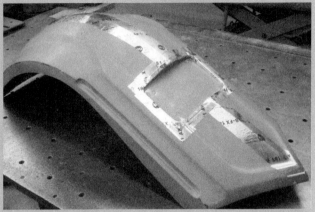

Narrowed fender is reassembled with metal backed insulation tape, on both sides. Tape will be scuffed and glued over.

Mock up of mounted bags after 2 inches are trimmed from the vertical dimension so they better fit the bike.

Here's an early test fit of the narrowed fender and the shortened bags all bolted in place.

They call these bikes custom for a reason, Rob had to take two inches out of the rear fender.

To finish the fender Rob formed panels from aluminum and used clecos to hold them in place initially.

Cindy's Softail

Once he's sure of the fitment, the aluminum panels are glued to the fender with 3M body panel adhesive.

The design evolves. At this point it's just a hood, with a Sharpie line where the turn signal housings will go.

Simple looking, the panels were hard to form. 16 gauge steel was mostly wheeled, edges were rolled over a fixture.

Nearly finished nacelle, with a 5-3/4 Daylighter from H-D. Blinkers will be LEDs.

Test fit for right side panel, which needs to fit the frame and the fender. Note wire edge, from 1/8th inch rod, of the whole panel to create a finished edge.

Unfinished, but you can see the profile - 26 inch RC front wheel, stretched tank, one-off side covers and unique fender and bags. Not your standard Softail.

More progress, dash is installed, along with the complete front fork assembly with 23 inch wheel and fender.

Underside gives some idea how much work went into just this relatively small piece. Again, note the edges finished with round rod.

Here you can see the hand-fabricated dash..

Factory fuel pump assembly bolts right into the tank. Threaded bung was added to provide a mounting point for the new dash.

...which requires more than one test fit.

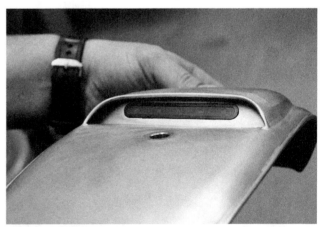

Stock indicator lights are built into the new dash and will plug right into the factory harness.

Another progress shot, complete with front wheel, fender, and side covers.

The new taillight is a stock unit meant to fit a 2014 Sportster. License mounting pad is an unusual size, Canadian license plates are a different size than those used in the US.

The 23 inch front wheel from PMFR was custom cut and machined to match the design of the H-D rear wheel.

Much of the sheet metal welding of the dash and tank is done with a TIG and silicon bronze rod, which requires less heat and thus minimizes warpage.

Nicely rounded side covers, fabricated from mild steel...

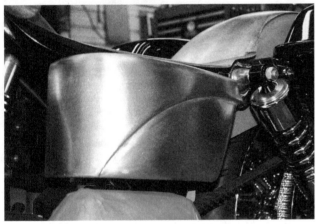

...complete with Rob's signature body lines.

The complete painted gas tank with H-D caps and fuel gauge, and reworked fuel injection cover.

Out in public for the first time prior to paint. Before final paint it's always a good idea to get a new bike outside or into a room big enough that the design and lines can be judged from a distance.

Final assembly underway. Note the lengths to which the crew goes in order to protect all that fresh paint.

Factory bags are retained, stock except for the nice paint.

Hand fabricated handle bars contain the factory Dyna speedo.

Because the frame was left black, the decision was made to include some black in the new paint job by Brian at Paint Works. Silver graphics are the work of Lenni at Krazy Kolors.

Dan's goal was a laid back sporty road bike. Something that looked good, and still fast enough to be fun to ride. The first part of that equation was addressed by Rob and crew at Donnie Smith Custom Cycles. The go fast part was taken care of when Dan dropped in a 120R TC from H-D.

Photos by: Dan Roche, Timothy Remus, Rob Roehl and Deb Shade

51

Chapter Four

Air Dam Sequence

Rob Roehl builds a Damn Spoiler

It's our good fortune to watch a master fabricator exercise his skills and build another custom part. Rob Roehl has been fabricating parts for years at Donnie Smith Custom Cycles, in Blaine, Minnesota. Rob's one-off air dam is the last piece of custom sheet metal needed to finish the work on Dan's Dyna.

Because of all the projects that are under way in the shop at the same time, I'm always amazed at how organized the guys are. Today was no different. Eager to share his process Rob was prepared to work.

If we back up for a moment to look at the position of the dam, we can see that the regulator

A simple shape proves not so easy to shape. Like most fabrication projects, this one starts in cardboard and morphs slowly into carefully shaped sheet metal.

is secured to a bracket - and that the air dam will bolt to that same bracket.

The bracket had to be made first of course, and once that was accomplished, Rob was able to begin designing the air dam. He uses cardstock to create the basic shape - it's firm enough to keep its shape, yet pliable enough to create bends - and magnets to hold his template in place, a mock air dam is born.

Prior to beginning the metal fabrication Rob gathered up all the tools he'll need for the job. This is an efficient way to account for necessities and at the same time visually inspect them for possible damage. Then he's ready to grab a sheet of steel and customize.

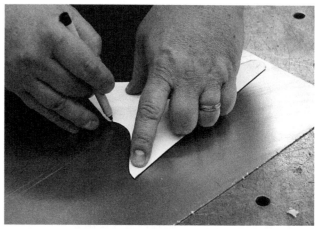

Rob creates a mock air dam with tag board, Fitting the template to the bike is easily done with magnets. The pattern is then traced with a Sharpie onto a sheet of 3303 H-14 aluminum.

The sheet metal needs to be deburred before any welding starts.

Next, using a band saw, Rob carefully cuts out all of the pieces he'll need to form the air dam.

Here are the 2 sides and the top of the air dam. Notice that the one piece has beveled edges.

The bead roller is a very useful tool. Each edge is run through as shown. Tight corners will need to be done by hand. Tooling can be changed depending upon the shape your need.

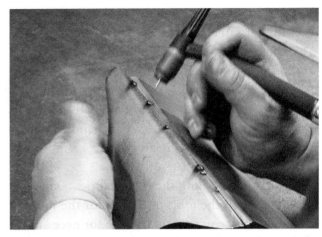

Now ready to tack, Rob holds the edges to line up the metal.

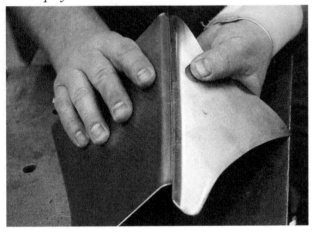

Rob tests the fit between the panels. You may have to roll it a few times until you get the fit you're looking for.

It's important that the seams don't overlap.

A rubber mallet and a T-dolly are used to roll the beveled edge at the corners.

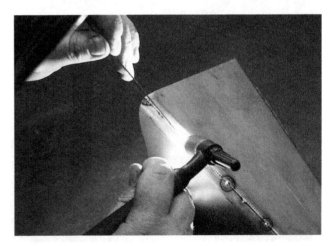

Tack welds are done quickly and spaced evenly along the seam.

Rob checks the fit of the air dam on the bracket.

The air dam is flipped upside down so he can trace a line along the inside.

An angle finder helps check each side for symmetry. A piece of paper could be used if an angle finder isn't handy.

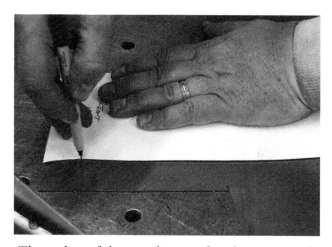

The outline of the stencil is transferred to a piece of sheet metal, the sheet is cut out on the band saw, and then the shaping can begin.

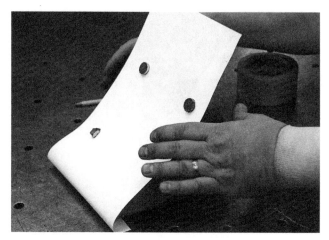

Now that the bottom and sides are together it's back to the tag board for the next stencil. Again Rob utilizes his magnets to create a snug fit as he traces out the air dam cover.

As before, sometimes there's no tool like a T-dolly and a leather-covered slapper.

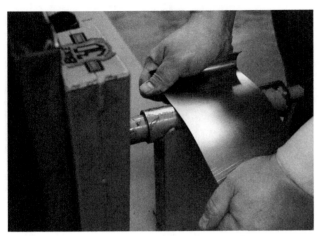

A curve begins to form as Rob shapes the sheet by hand.

Rob spreads out the tack welds so as not to concentrate too much heat. Less heat means less chance of warpage.

It's important to check the fit of the seams before you tack it. Remember, the edges can't overlap, the two pieces should butt together at the seam.

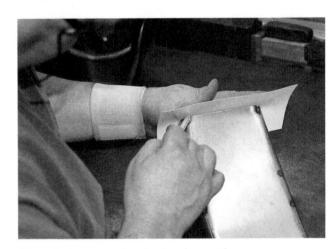

Now Rob can make the final stencil.

Once he's happy with the fit, Rob begins tack welding the piece in place.

A washer of the right size is used as a template for the nose.

This small piece is best formed by hand with the T-dolly and the slap hammer.

Time to ensure the air dam fits the bracket. Note the slot in the front, intended to make sure there's plenty of fresh, cool air for the regulator.

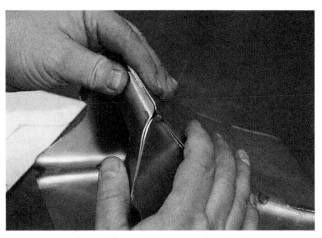

Rob stops often to check the fit.

The air dam has had it's final fit and is ready to be welded. Rob will work tirelessly behind his welding helmet to achieve optimal welds.

The air damn is formed, tacked together and ready to be fitted one last time.

The finished air dam - the welding complete and all seams metal finished. All it needs now is paint.

Photos and copy by Deb Shade

Chapter Five

TIG Welding

Rob Roehl walks us through TIG Basics

ROB'S TIG WELDING TIPS

To start with, knowledge of the machine is paramount. You have to know how to determine the best temperature and speed. Which means you have to know the thickness of the material. You also need to match the diameter of the rod to the thickness of the material. With the temperature, I like to start low. In terms of how fast you should weld, the speed, it's all about getting a feel for it.

With a MIG it's all about a blast of heat and speed - crank it up until it sounds like frying bacon. That does not work with a TIG.

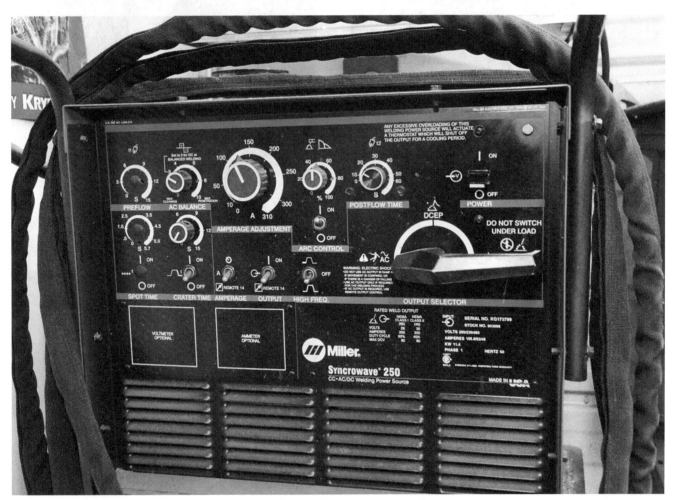

Rob's Miller 250 Syncrowave with a water-cooled torch is a great all around welder for both steel and aluminum.

When I teach people to TIG weld, I tell them, "It's like driving a car and it requires practice. The pedal is like a gas pedal, on a nice day you might have it on the floor, but when you're driving in snow, not so much."

As a rule of thumb, I set the welder at 50 to 100 amps for almost any sheet metal, (14 gauge for example). And always remember that when you add rod you cool the puddle.

When you are TIG welding sheet metal, you don't need a lot of rod, just enough to get it going. Every 2 or 3 steps you add a little rod. It's kind of like a dance. There's a rhythm you need to discover.

Dipping the filler rod into the weld puddle takes some practice, trial and error. Adding too much creates excessive buildup, too little and your weld will be under cut or you end up with blowouts.

People talk about fusion welds, a weld done without adding any rod, they can be used but it can also be challenging. I still want to see some backside weld even though it's ugly.

ALUMINUM

With thicker aluminum it's hard to get complete penetration, especially with shaped parts, without creating warpage from the heat. With thinner material penetration isn't such a problem, but it's best to look at the backside cracks and to judge the penetration. Even if all you do is fusion weld the backside, you end up with the same amount of weld and stress and on both sides.

With aluminum, you can't weld hot enough to get really good penetration on the whole thing. You just can't put that much heat in, so I weld both sides. if it's .080 or .090 inch material, I will have some gaps, then I have to add some filler. Some guys anneal it to relieve the stress, but if you weld both sides you probably don't have to do the annealing.

WHAT'S IT GOING TO BE?

Always consider what the part is going to be, a fender, a gas tank or a simple skirt. That dictates a lot how I weld and what I weld it with. I consider things like: will it hold a liquid, is it a stressed member, does it need to be metal finished, will it be painted or chrome plated?

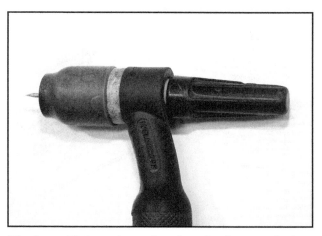

The basic TIG torch, with a short back-cap, which makes it easier to get into tight areas to weld.

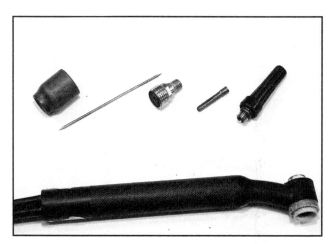

The basic components of the torch: Ceramic nozzle, tungsten, gas lens, collet and back-cap.

Rob likes the lower, larger lens, "the screen, makes all the difference, it disperses the gas better. Most guys use this just for alum, but it's really good on tubing, the gas follows the arc around. I just leave it in the torch all the time. For me it works good - period."

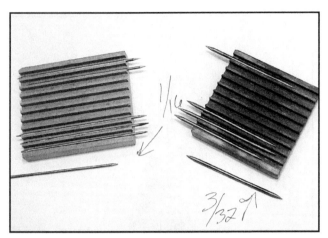

Tungstens come in different diameters, "I use 3/32 inch for nearly everything, 1/16 only for very thin material."

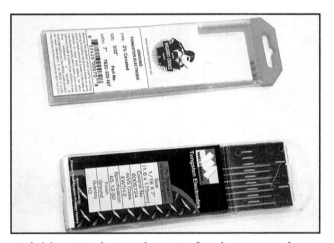

Rob likes 2% thoriated, uses it for almost everything, but adds, "the 2% ceriated starts soft, you don't have to feed it so much power right away to get it started. It's good for thinner material."

A basic welding sequence with two pieces of 16 gauge sheet steel. A nice tight fit is important, "no gap is better than any gap."

In the case of decorative work, I love silicon-bronze. It welds way cooler, more like gluing something together. People try to really weld with silicon-bronze, but it's more like soldering. It melts at a lower temperature and sometimes it's the best option.

CHOOSING A ROD

Most of the time you have to know what you are welding. Sometimes it's a case of dis-similar metals. Stainless steel rod works good for this, like when you are welding stainless to steel for example, or when you're welding chrome moly to mild steel. For welding aluminum I use two different rods, 4043 or 5356, both are common alloys. 4043 is the weld-all. It works on most aluminum alloys, but you have to understand there are alloys of aluminum that are un-weldable. So know what the alloy is first. 4043 seems to be a good catch-all, though it may not be a perfect color match for cast aluminum.

A better color match for something like a chipped fin on a motor is 5356 rod.

For mild steel I use ER70S-2. It's my mild steel go-to rod. I've also been using "weld mold 880," it has a higher tensile strength than the ER70-2, and some of the properties of stainless rod. I use it for frame work and tubing, not for sheet metal.

PREPARATION

I think the importance of prep can't be overemphasized. The parts must fit together perfectly, no gap is ideal. The material needs to be clean at the seam, and with heavier material you need to bevel the edges before doing any welding.

FINAL WORDS OF WISDOM

You know, I can teach you how to weld in five minutes, but it takes the next 10 years to get it right. The pedal, your brain and your hands all have to be coordinated. Getting that rhythm I mentioned earlier, that is the whole key. When I taught my son to TIG weld, I said, "you're a drummer, you get timing, just find the right pace."

The process starts with two tack welds. Power is set at 50 amps, the argon is adjusted to 18 psi, "remember that argon cools the weld so you don't want more than you need."

The weld itself is done in three short sections. The rod I'm using is the same diameter as the thickness of the material.

The technique used is a little different on each of the three welded areas.

Q&A: Rob Roehl

For over twenty years, Rob Roehl has done everything from extending fenders to fabricating complete motorcycle tanks at Donnie Smith Custom Cycles. And we all know, you can't do good fabrication without good welding skills, the two go hand in hand. So in this case we've asked Rob to share with us what he knows about that other skill - TIG welding.

Rob, how did you get started welding and fabricating?

I started out young, helping my Dad work on his race boat, I think I was in my teens. You couldn't buy any race parts at that time, so we had to make everything. That's where it stated, and of course I made models as a kid.

After the Marine Corps I started work at Hoffman Engineering, that's where I got certified as a welder. That was all MIG welding,

but I learned the basics of welding there. And then about twenty years ago I started to hang around Donnie Smith's shop. I had my first Harley, and when I stopped by Donnie would always get me to help him with some project.

Pretty soon I quit the job at Hoffman and started working for Donnie. He had a TIG machine so that's when I started TIG welding. Donnie taught me the basics, but then I met Don Ness (famed pro-street chassis builder), his shop was right across the parking lot from ours. Don and his crew really taught me a lot. How to be a better TIG welder, how to work with tubing, and how to make sure my welds had good penetration. They took my welding skills to the next level.

How about your fabrication skills, did you take any classes for that?

I took a couple of Ron Covell's seminars, but that's all, I have no formal training. But again, Donnie and Don Ness taught me a lot. Besides the two of them I received a ton of help and encouragement from Loren Richards. Don Ness and Loren were the best mentors I could have hoped for. Without their help I would have just gotten by, but they helped me achieve a higher level of proficiency. They showed me what I was capable of, and they made me more efficient. One of the things they showed me was how I could fabricate pretty amazing parts with simple tools. You don't need a power hammer or power shrinker, just simple tools and basic knowledge - and a willingness to take on the job.

I think too, as a whole, I benefitted from the progression of bikes I've built. We started building relatively rudimentary machines. Then, during the last boom, we started building bikes with budgets that were off the chart.

Q&A: Rob Roehl

So that was a good motivator and an opportunity for me. People were willing to spend the money, there was money for high-end fabrication, and the industry was hungry to see new designs.

Let's go back to talking about pure welding. What do people miss when they first learn TIG welding?

People think they can just sit down and pick it up right away, and they worry about how fast they are. But they need to really stick with the basics. They need to have an understanding of what they're doing. New welders need to focus on the essentials, melting the metal and adding enough rod, and doing each of those separate things at the right pace. I call it a dance. Ultimately what you're trying to do is make a good durable weld.

What's the hardest thing about learning TIG?

The hardest thing is having the patience to practice and practice. You have to have a certain oddball coordination - even when you're in a funny position.

Any final words of wisdom?

Take the time to do the preparation correctly and thoroughly. If you have time to do the welding you have the time to clean and prep the surfaces as needed. New TIG welders forget that TIG is more sensitive to impurities than other types of welding. It's not an arc welder that will blast through almost anything.

I consider myself pretty a good welder, but I still work at my welding, trying to make it better, every time I weld something.

The verbatim note Rob provided when asked to provide a written list of the important things to remember when TIG welding.

The Really Important Shit
1. Know your equipment.
2. Know your materials.
3. Know the application.
4. Match the filler rod to the job, i.e. the material type.
5. Use the Proper heat range for the job.
6. Prep the work, it must fit together correctly.
7. Bevel if necessary.
8. Weld both sides (Always???)
9. Size the filler rod to the thickness of the material.
10. Match tungsten to the job.
11. Always clean the materials before welding.
12. Speed = heat + thickness.
13. Consider the end finish, i.e. plated, painted or??
14. Consider Stress on the finished part, and longevity.
15. Clean it once more before starting to weld.

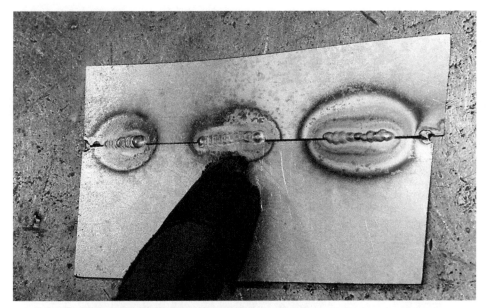

Checking the penetration of the weld by examining the back side of the welds. The center weld shows good even penetration. With the weld on the right I used too much rod on purpose - which cools off the weld and affects penetration.

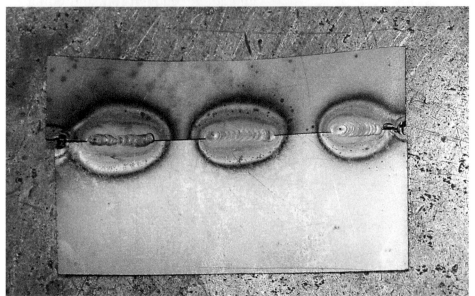

The front side shows pretty much the same story. Note the cold weld on the far left where I used too much rod. On the right side I used too much heat and not enough rod. The middle weld is good with just enough of both heat and rod.

Here's our right angle example. "I tack it first. but it pulls to the side I'm welding from, so I have to tack both ends on both sides."

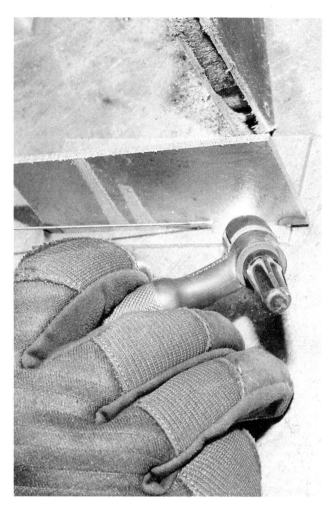

1) I start by tack welding the back side...

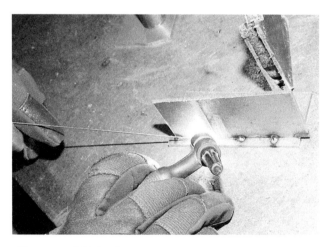

2)...every 3/4 inch or so.

3) Now I can start the weld...

4) ...adding rod as necessary.

5) This is a nice even bead.

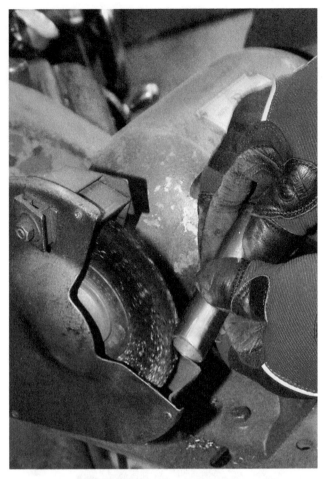

1) Before welding the tubing I clean the slag and burs off the edge...

3) This is the first tack...

4) ...the second tack goes on the other side.

2) ...next I check the fit, note the slight bevel left from the last step.

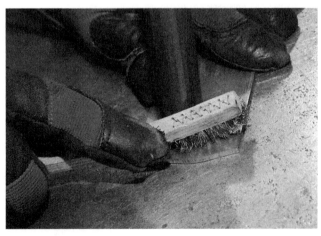

5) It's a good idea to clean the gap with a wire brush before starting the actual welding.

1) I begin the weld...

2) ...and gradually work my way...

4) A nice looking finished weld. The tubing is .120 inch wall thickness and the plate measures 1/8 inch thick.

3) ...all the way around.

5) The bottom shows a good heat pattern.

Especially with aluminum, the two surfaces must be super clean. I like to start with a wire brush, then I use lacquer thinner and a rag.

I start the tack welding with a 4043 rod, AC/DC control on AC, balance at 5, about 125 amps.

Welding the front after all the tacking is done. This material is about .090 inches thick.

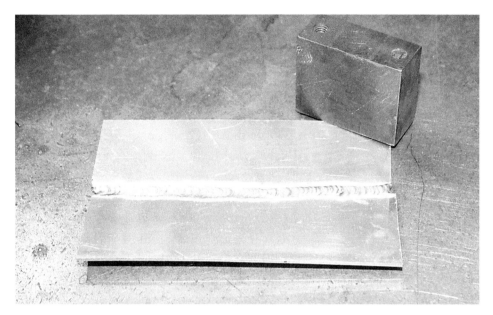

This is the top side weld, note the warpage.

A little work with a hammer and it's flat again.

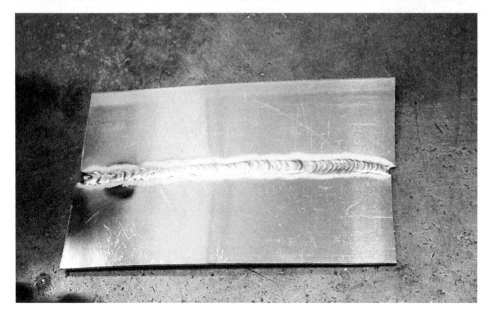

I fusion welded the back side, then will have to work it with the hammer to eliminate the warpage.

Copy and captions by Rob Roehl

Buying Your First TIG

TIG welders are no longer so big and so expensive that only a busy commercial shop can consider buying one. Today there are affordable TIG welders ideally suited to home-based and small commercial shops. To help make sense of what's available we spent a little time with Steve Lundborg, branch manager for Mississippi Welders Supply, a regional 10-store chain selling welding equipment of all types.

Steve: First, let's talk briefly about TIG. What, exactly, is it about a TIG that makes it a better welder than a MIG or a gas setup?

A TIG (tungsten inert gas) is better than MIG (metal inert gas) for a number of reasons. The TIG will have a smaller heat affected zone and you can control the heat more precisely. Also, the better ones have a pulse mode to freeze the puddle, and give you a better bead appearance. Pulse is also nice to have for welding stainless steel. But the one biggest reason people like TIG welders is because of the relatively small heat affected zone.

It seems that smaller TIG welders are coming down in price, so that it's easier for someone at home or in a small shop to buy one, is that true?

Yes, there are more small, relatively inexpensive TIGs available than there were a few years ago. This is partly because of the inverter technology. The smaller machines use an inverter instead of a transformer. The inverter power sources are smaller, more efficient, and they're lighter so the whole machine is lighter.

What is the price range for smaller units, and what do I get as I go up from the least expensive to one that costs a bit more. What do I get if I spend some extra money?

Thermal Arc makes a DC-only machine that's only about $1100.00. It's inverter based, but because it has no AC it's only good for welding steel and stainless, you can't weld aluminum. The Thermal Arc can also be used as a stick welder, so it's versatile, runs on 110 or 220 volts and only weighs about ten pounds. We've sold a lot of those to pipe fitters, they like them because they're so small and have the stick welding ability. A Thermal Arc would also work well for a small shop

Though it has no AC option, the Thermal Arc has the big advantage of compact size combined with a relatively compact price tag.

Buying Your First TIG

if you didn't need the AC option.

If you can spend a little more money, Miller has their Diversion series. The model 180 is an inverter machine, and it runs on 220 or 110 volts. This machine is DC and AC (AC for aluminum) and costs about $1800. If you move up to Miller's Dynasty series, you get all of the above, with more power and the pulse mode.

One step up from the Thermal Arc, the Diversion 180 has both a DC and AC setting.

Let's talk a little about gas welding. Everyone wants a MIG or TIG, is a gas-welding outfit a viable alternative for general shop-type welding?

We still sell gas outfits, but we just don't have much call for them anymore.

I understand there is a difference in the shielding gas used for TIG, as opposed to what is used for MIG?

Yes, with a TIG the gas is straight argon, (no matter the metal being welded). But with a MIG, the gas is a blend, 75% argon and 25% CO_2. So you have to be careful when you have the tank filled.

If I buy a TIG welder where do I learn how to use it, do shops like yours offer classes?

We don't provide classes, but most community colleges and tech schools do offer evening and summer classes for adults including a variety of welding classes. The closest school for us is WITC in New Richmond, Wisconsin. I'm sure though that you can find a similar program in any state.

In terms of brands what do you like to see people buy, and what do you think they should avoid.

Well, we sell Miller and Thermal Arc. Both are US companies, both are supported by stores like ours so you know you can get service and parts if there's any kind of problem. I always tell people to avoid the cheap off-shore units, because generally they are not well supported, so if you have a problem down the road, or you need parts, you might be out of luck.

Chapter Six

Machining 101

How-to: Vertical Mill and Lathe Operation

THE MIGHTY BRIDGEPORT

What most of us call a "Bridgeport" is really a vertical mill. As Kurt Senescal from Creative Metalworks explains, "A lathe just spins things, so you can make them round. With a mill, you can make square parts or round parts, there are just so many more things you can do with a Bridgeport."

It's easy to understand how Bridgeport became the generic name that most of us associate with any vertical mill, as there seems to be a true Bridgeport in the vast majority of fabrication and repair shops where we hang out - shops dedicated

For a lot of motorheads, there is no such thing as a "vertical mill." But there is this terrific machine seen in all the shops and it's called a Bridgeport.

to the repair and construction of hot rods, of all types and flavors.

It was 1938 when the first Bridgeports, manufactured in Bridgeport, Connecticut, were introduced. To say they were successful is an understatement. Even after other manufacturers of machine tools began to offer similar features, Bridgeport remained the dominant brand for small and medium-sized machine shops.

Today, most true machine shops and manufacturing plants have switched to automated equipment, the ubiquitous CNC machines, which means that the original, manual Bridgeport machines can be found and had for anywhere from $500 to $2500. Like all used equipment, price differences between one machine and another are mostly due to condition, age and features. Among the available features offered through the years, by far the most popular is variable speed. To change the RPM of the tool in a manual machine, it's necessary to stop the machine, take the tension off the belt (see the nearby photos) and chose a different set of pulleys to either increase of decrease the speed of the tool. Variable-speed machines use an adjustable pulley, the diameter of which (and thus the RPM) can be changed on the fly while the machine is running.

Whether the Bridgeport in question uses the manual pulley system or the variable speed pulley, they all have a two-speed clutch hub. in either case, the RPM can be adjusted from 80 to over 2000 RPM (more on tool speed a little later).

Unlike the variable speed option, all Bridgeport mills come with a head assembly that can be rotated on the vertical axis, as well as rotated (angled) around a horizontal axis. The head assembly can also be angled back and forth, relative to the angle of the operator (see nearby photos).

The bed itself can also be moved in three axis, X, Y and Z (up and down); power feed options can be had for both the X and Y movement. In addition, there are a whole host of options, like rotary tables and DRO panels (digital read out).

A Bridgeport is simply one hell of a machine, with patience and a little creativity there aren't many machining tasks you can't tackle.

Changing the tooling on a Bridgeport starts by appling the brake then loosening the drawbar. The drawbar screws into the collet or tool holder (see pics below)...

... next, you need to tap on the top of the drawbar with a brass or rubber hammer - never, never use a steel hammer on a Bridgeport.

Now the collet and the tool itself will drop out.

Once the collet is pulled out, the drawbar can be removed as shown - you do not normally need to pull the drawbar all the way out to remove a collet.

The various belt pulleys, and an integral two-speed hub, make it possible to change the speed of the tool from 80 to over 2000 RPM.

Reinstalling the drawbar starts by hand tightening the nut on top...

To move the belt to a different set of pulleys, start by loosening the motor locknut handle, and moving the motor on it's pivot, which takes the tension off the belt .....

... then the final tightening can be done while holding the brake. Tightening the drawbar pulls the tapered collet up into the quill, forcing it to grip the tool.

... then switch to the new belt position...

... put tension on the belt and lock the motor in place with the motor locknut handle.

Moving the table along the y axis (closer or farther away from you) is done with the handle on the front of the machine.

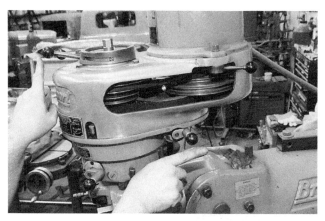

Changing from hi to low range is done by moving the two levers shown here, together is low, apart is hi. When going to hi range it's necessary to spin the chuck so you know the gears are engaged.

The third handle, shown here, moves the table along the z axis, (up and down).

The table can be moved along the x axis (to the left and right) with the crank handle as shown.

The mill can be used as a drill press by moving the quill up and down with the handle, or you can engage the power feed.

To stop the quill at a certain point, an adjustable stop can be set. In manual mode, the stop will physically stop the movement of the quill. In powered mode, the stop will kick the power feed out of gear.

If on the other hand, you don't want the quill to move at all the lock shown here can be engaged.

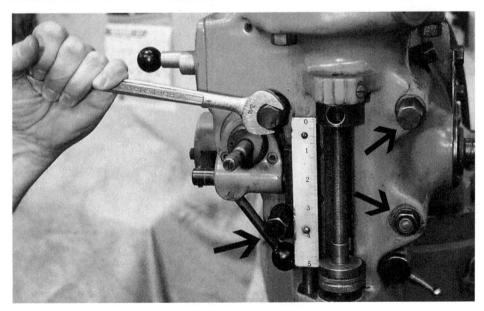

The Bridgeport was a big hit when first introduced partly because it is so very flexible. The four bolts shown here can be loosened...

2).... as shown.

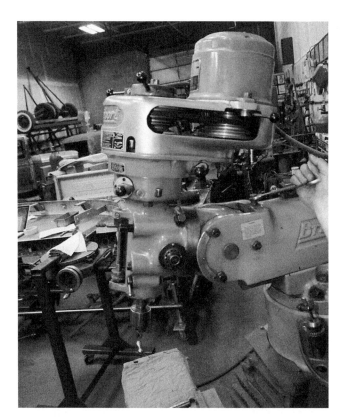

4) ... and use the adjustment (note Kurt's hand) to tilt the head as shown.

1) ... then the adjustment seen here can be used to pivot the head of the mill on the horizontal axis...

3) Or, you can loosed the three bolt heads on the side of the mill...

5) With the bolts shown here (there are a total of 4) you can slide the whole head assembly forward and back with the handle.

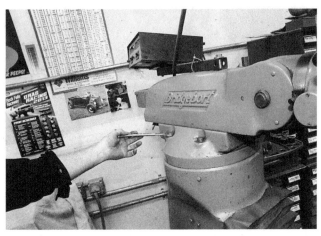

1) You can also turn the turret on the vertical axis by loosening the bolts shown (again, there are 4)...

2) ... then swinging the turret manually.

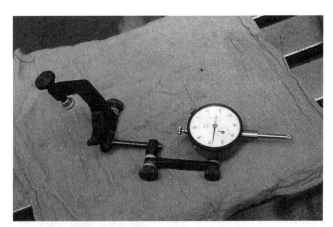

3) All this swinging and jiving might leave you wondering if the head is really perpendicular to the table... in which case you need to "indicate the table," which is done with an indecol (the holding fixture) and a dial indicator...

4) ... the indecol allows you to mount the dial indicator to the quill as shown.

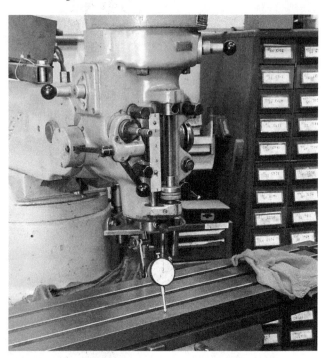

5) You should be able to rotate the dial indicator through a 360 degree rotation, in 90 degree increments, and see no change in the reading. "This can be very time consuming," warns Kurt.

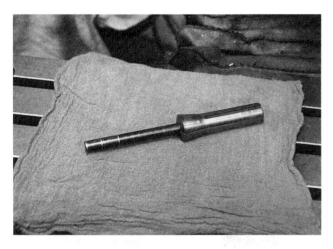

1) There is a simpler way to indicate the table. This Plan B, which starts with a piece of perfectly straight drill rod mounted in the collet...

3) Start the process with the dial indicator at the very end of the drill rod.

2) ... and the collet mounted in the mill, with the indecol and dial indicator set up as shown.

4) Now, use the big crank handle on the front of the mill to move the table up (on the z axis).

5) The reading on the dial indicator should remain constant as you raise the table. This Plan B method is much easier than the original Plan A.

With the head indicated, you need to indicate the vise, which only needs to be done on the x axis - i.e. take a reading at one end of the vise, and move the table until you get a reading at the other end.

Half the job of milling is just mounting the material to be milled to the table. Luckily there are kits like the one shown, that make it relatively easy to securely mount odd shapes.

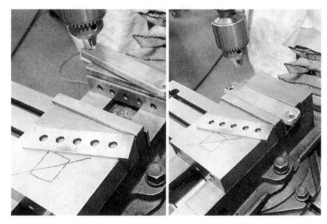

Parallels are often used to provide a machined shoulder for the work to sit on, squeezed securely by the jaws of the vise.

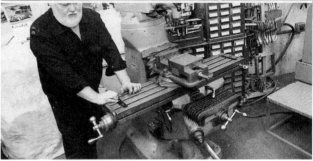

When checking the condition of a mill, be sure to check the amount of play in the table (when it's not locked in place). Some of the play can be adjusted out, but if it's too bad the sliding surfaces must be machined true.

Checking for play in the quill is a simple matter of extending it all the way and then moving it back and forth.

The speed of the quill power feed is variable, adjusted by the crank seen here.

Push-Pull

Lever

The lower lever is used to engage the power feed for the quill, while the upper push-pull control is used to change the direction of feed.

A variety of collets are needed for a variety of tools. Each ID matches the shaft OD of a particular tool.

For drilling a chuck can be mounted to a collet and then inserted into the mill.

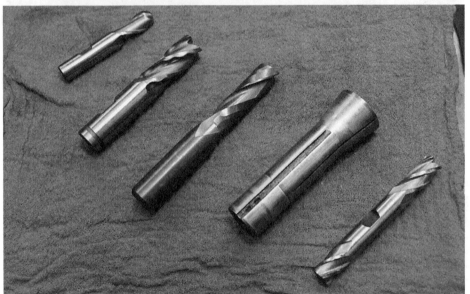

Some common tools include (top left to bottom right) a ball-end mill, a roughing or hogging mill, a 2-flute mill, a collet and a 4-flute mill.

Close up shows a collet holding a 4-flute end mill. The taper matches the female taper of the quill, pulling the collet up into position with the drawbar tightens the collet's grip on the tool.

A rotary table adds considerably to the already long list of things you can make and shape with a Bridgeport.

Center the table under the quill, add one end mill and you can make a step in the work, as shown, just by rotating the table as the end mill spins.

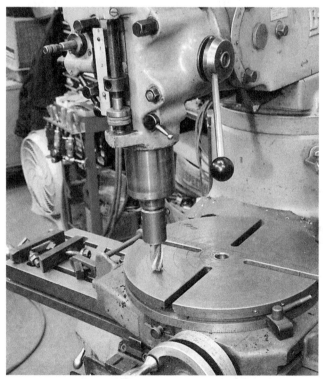

Locate the rotary table mounted off-center relative to the centerline of the quill, and the possibilities are almost endless.

The line drawn on the aluminum plate shows the path the end mill will follow as the table (and the work) rotate.

The Lathe

While the vertical mill is a somewhat modern tool, the lathe is at least 3000 years old - some of the very first examples were powered by one person pulling a rope wrapped around the piece of work while the second person shaped the wood with a sharp tool. Eventually the power-person was replaced by belts driven by a water wheel or horses, and later, steam.

Though it might be true that lathes are only good for making things round, there are actually three operations commonly performed on a lathe: turning, facing and boring.

Compared to a Bridgeport, lathes are fairly simple machines. On one end you have the headstock, the heart and soul of a lathe. The headstock contains the engine or drive mechanism that rotates the spindle. Whether through belts or gears or a variable-speed motor, the headstock has provisions to change the speed of the spindle, the device that holds the work.

Most spindles use a three-jaw chuck to secure and center the work, though four jaw spindles are a nice option for mounting items that have a rectangular or irregular shape. When the work is mounted in the lathe with a chuck, it's a good idea to do as many operations as possible without removing the work from the machine. Because anytime you take a shaft or object out of the jaws, and then put it back in later, there will be some shift in the position, and you will have to indicate the work again before you go back to cutting.

The tailstock, as the name suggests, is located at the other end of the bed from the headstock, and is generally used as a place to mount a center and thus help to support the work at the other end. For metal work, a live center with a high quality bearings is often used in the tailstock to support the work (note the photos).

Your basic metal-cutting lathe with headstock, tailstock and tool support or carriage.

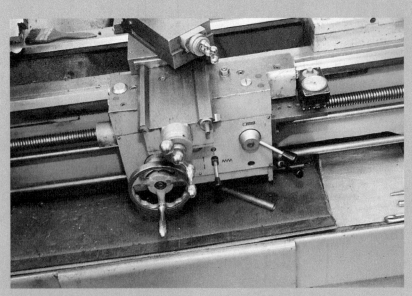

The tool support can be moved manually with the lowest/largest wheel, or the power drive. The cross slide can likewise be moved manually or by power drive.

The tailstock can be equipped with a chuck for a drill bit as seen here, or more often, a shaft with a tapered end used as a support for the work.

The tool holder in this case is from Aloris, which makes for fast tool changes.

Not all lathes are the same, this Harris lathe uses the levers seen here to change the speed of the spindle.

Between the headstock and the tailstock is the bed, with precision slots that allow both the carriage and tailstock to move parallel to the centerline of the headstock. The carriage is gear driven by the long screw gear seen on most lathes that moves the tool parallel to the work, or axially. There is also a cross slide mechanism in the carriage that allows the tool holder to be moved radially, closer to or farther away from the work. Both these movements can be done manually with the wheels seen on the front of the tool support, or with a variable speed power feed.

Shown in the nearby photos is an Aloris tool holder with its quick release feature so the part of the toolholder that actually clamps the tool can be quickly pulled off the lathe and another clamped in its place.

Operation

With the lathe, the important thing to keep in mind is not just the RPM of the spindle, but the surface speed of the work. If the work is a small

The lower levers control the speed and direction of the power feed.

The Aloris tool holder does more than just hold the tool. Loosen two nuts and the mechanism rotates.

The part of the tool holder that actually holds the tool or can be popped off quickly by just...

diameter rod the effective surface speed is much faster than that of a larger diameter piece running at the same spindle RPM.

Tools

Most fab shops, including Creative Metalworks, buy lathe bit blanks, and shape them as needed for a particular job. "The cutting bit needs to be higher at the tip," explains Kurt, "that's all. We sharpen and shape them for each particular job."

Cutting fluid

Whether you're working on the mill or the lathe, there are plenty of times when the operation will require cutting oil. Cutting oil is more a coolant than an aid to the actual cutting. With aluminum Kurt just blows compressed air at the tool to provide cooling and help clear the chips away from the work.

... twisting the handle shown here in a counter-clockwise direction. The nice thing about this is you have 5 or 6 different bits ready to drop on at a moment's notice.

A good way to ensure the cutting edge will contact the work on the horizontal centerline - a thin piece of metal should be vertical when held against the work by the edge of the tool bit.

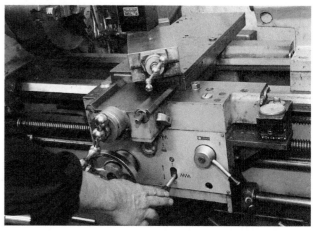

Shown is the control for the horizontal feed. Just above that is the feed control at 90 degrees to the lathe's axis.

A center is simply a support with a pointed end that supports the "other end" of the work. A live center like this one is equipped with a bearing.

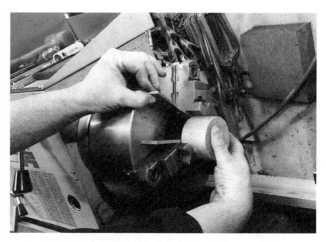

For mounting round objects like that shown, a set of parallels are often used to keep the work square.

If a piece of work is taken out of the lathe, then reinstalled, it needs to be indicated with the dial indicator as shown. Sometimes a tap from a soft hammer is all that's required to bring it in line.

At Creative Metalworks, and most fabrication shops, tool blanks are shaped to fit the job at hand, these are just a few examples.

Chapter Seven

Materials

Raw Stock for your Shop

One of the things that you need to do as you set up your shop at home is decide what type of materials to keep in the shop for your building projects or for use for modifications and repairs. It really depends on if this is a new shop and you need to make some work tables, welding benches, stands, and also fixtures to hang stuff in your new shop. Then, after your shop is setup and all this is done, are you going to be working on just motorcycles or are you going to be working on other things in your shop? It is always nice to keep some materials for building another bench or some

Here I am checking the tubing, and the information stamped on each piece.

other type of fixture.

The first thing to realize is when you order materials is what the description is to be sure you are ordering the right part. This not only saves the grief when you get your order that you have received the correct material, but will make it much easier on the sales person. This way the next time you place an order with the company you already have established a good relationship with the sales staff. What I mean is, know the meanings of flat bar, square bar, round bar and angle iron. Then, know the meanings of the tubing descriptions. Is it round, square, rectangular or streamline? What is 1018, A-36, 1020, DOM, seamless and what is 4130? There is so much to know that hopefully I will be able to walk you through the descriptions of the different shapes, materials and their uses. Hopefully you will have a better understanding of the characteristics of the metals and shapes and what their best usages are.

Know the correct shape and material for what you are building and what kind of stress it will experience. Be sure you know the characteristics of each of the materials. What is the material's strength, weld-ability, machine-ability and can it be formed or bent?

So let's first going over names of the shapes.

The first shape will be flat stock. This also goes by a few other names, such as flat bar or rectangular bar. It

A great selection of flat stock. Note the fact that all the pieces carry a color code on the end.

A huge selection of 1018 cold-rolled mild steel.

is one of the most widely used shapes. It can be used as a flat material, which if needed, also can be shaped by bending or machining. It is a solid piece of material. An example would be ¼ inch thick with a width of 4 inches.

Next will be square bar. Square bar is a piece of metal that is exactly like the name implies, square. It is a solid piece of material. An example of square bar would be 1 inch x 1 inch

Round bar is a piece of round stock and this material is solid. If the description says bar, this means that it is a piece of solid material. This material is sized by diameter. An example would be ¾ inch round bar.

Angle steel, sometimes called angle iron, is shaped with 2 flat surfaces at an angle of 90 degrees. Very useful structurally for building benches, jigs, and many other uses in a home shop. The sides of the angle can be equal in size. An example would be 2 inch x 2 inch x ¼ inch thick angle or the angle can have different length sides. An example of that would be 2 inch x 3 inch x 1/4 inch thick.

Next I want to talk to you about tubing. What is the difference between tubing and pipe? Pipe is used for a vessel for liquids or gases. It goes by pipe sizes that refer to the inside diameter. It is not rated in yield strengths but in pressures measured in pounds per square inch (PSI). Pipe goes by schedule numbers and not by wall thickness. I will explain yield strength further ahead in this article. Tubing is measured by O.D. (Outside Diameter) and by how thick the tube wall is. Tubing is made for structural work and the yield strengths and other important information is available, such as, ultimate tensile, yield strength, elongation and hardness. Again, I will tell you in detail what these numbers mean.

Tubing comes in many different shapes. It comes in round, square, rectangle and streamline. It is important to know that tubing sizes come with descriptions as decimal units. If you want a round tube 5/8 of an inch you need to order .625 inch tubing. Know your decimal descriptions when you place your order. If you want tubing with a wall thickness of 1/8 of an inch, order .125 inch wall thickness. This way when you place your order there is no chance of something getting converted wrong.

The round shape tubing is the most common shape used in motorcycle frames. It is measured by O.D. and by wall thickness. This wall thickness measurement again is in thousandths of an inch. This information along with other info is stamped on the tubing. It can be bent in any direction making a very versatile shape. Because of the round shape, it is the same strength and stiffness in any direction. Because of this it can flex when needed and relieve stresses in other areas. An example of round tubing would be 1 inch (diameter) x .049 inch (wall thickness).

The square tubing offers more stiffness and strength

Though motorcycle builders use a lot of round tubing, rectangular tube, and ...

in forces going against it across the flat faces. Forces at angles against the flats provide less strength vs round tubing. It can be bent against the flats but is harder to do than round tubing. An example would be 1.5 inch x 1.5 inch x .058 inch.

Rectangular tubes offer greater strength and stiffness against the longer width area. What I mean is, I have a section that is 2 inch x 1 inch x .083 inch . If the force is parallel to the 2 inch section it will be much stronger than going against the 1 inch section.

Streamline tubes are tubes made to be more aerodynamic. They usually have a ratio of 2.36 of the minor axis. The minor axis is the width. So if the minor axis is 1.00 inch then the major axis would be 1.00 inch x 2.36 = 2.36 inches. Streamline tubes, some call them teardrop or aero, but the proper name is streamline. Because of the shape it is a poor choice to be a strong structural tube. You need to check with who you are ordering from to see what sizes they keep in inventory. An example to order a streamline tube from Stock Car Steel and Aluminum would be part # SL23-10-4. This streamline tube will have a wall thickness of .049 inch. The major axis is 2.360 inch and the minor axis is 1.00 inch. It is not as confusing as you think once you check out their website.

So now that you know the names of the different shaped metals, what about how the material was formed into these shapes and different thicknesses?

The flat stock, square bar, round bar and angle can be formed either by hot rolled or cold rolled methods. The hot rolled will usually have some scale and a rougher appearance. Hot rolled is formed at a higher temperature and tolerances and finish are not as nice as the cold rolled method.

Cold rolled is done at a lower temperature resulting in a much nicer finish and tighter tolerances of measurements. Generally cold rolled tubing has stronger yield strength than the same material formed by the hot rolling method.

Tubing is made with two different methods. One method is DOM, which stands for Drawn Over Mandrel. This method starts out as flat stock which is formed into a tube and welded to make a seamed tube. There is no such thing as seamless DOM tubing. After being formed into the DOM tubing and welded, the tube is then heated above 1700f to normalize the tubing. This removes any built up stresses in the tubing that came about during the forming process. The tubing is then cold drawn several times until it gets down to the outside diameter and wall thickness for the tubing specifications. The cold working of the tubing makes the metal grain structure much finer and actually this cold working of the tube will make the seamed area undetectable. This makes the material stronger. DOM tubing is made with many different materials but the most common are 1020 steel and 4130.

The other method of making tubing is seam-

....square stock can be very useful for making supports and brackets.

less. It is made from billet material and rotary pierced as a tube. The tubing is then normalized and then cold worked several times in the same way DOM tubes are made. This cold working is done until the proper O.D. and wall thickness are achieved - cold working makes a fine-grain tube that is much stronger and has much tighter tolerances. Seamless tubes are readily available in 1018 and 4130 material.

So, what do these numbers mean that I mentioned in the paragraphs above? Let me first explain what certain numbers mean for the characteristics of different steels.

Tensile Strength, which some companies call, Ultimate Tensile Strength, is a measure of the stress required to bring a material to the point where it breaks - measured in PSI (Pounds per Square Inch) it takes for this failure. This "square inch" is a solid piece of material. When looking at these specifications, I like to see how much difference there is between the Ultimate Tensile Strength versus the Yield Strength of the material.

Yield Strength, I like to think of this as the material's working strength. This also is measured in PSI, but this time it's the amount of force or stress it takes to bend the material to the point where it retains the bent shape after the stress is removed. If a tube takes a big impact, past the yield point, it will cause the tube to actually buckle or ripple in that area where the most stress was seen by the tubing. As long as you stay under the yield strength of the material it will go back to its original location or shape. The important thing to remember is that if the material see a stress over the yield strength, all it did was bend, but that is not a failure as in a separation or crack, as happens when the force went over the tensile strength. An easy visualization of this is a paper clip. This paper clip you have on your desk could last you a lifetime. As long as you only use it to hold a few papers together it always comes back together to the shape it had was when you first used it. What happens when you get a huge stack of papers and use that same paper clip on them? The paper clip doesn't spring back together as before. The reason? You went past the yield strength of the steel used in that paper clip. So now you get your fingernail and bend it back straight, but the next time you use it, it now sticks out a little again. Once you go past the yield strength (working strength) you have lost some of the strength and memory the steel had before.

This is why I like to see a big difference between Yield Strength and Tensile strength. I would like to see the part or frame that I made to have been bent, ripple or buckle on the tubes versus a tube that has come apart with a complete failure! Materials where the tensile strength and yield strength are close together don't give that cushion of extra strength if needed.

The next specification the metal will have is elongation. This is how much the material will stretch

Rectangular and square tubing comes in many sizes with many different wall thicknesses.

before failure. This is an important specification when you compare materials. If the tubing gets a dent in it, did the elongation cause any stress cracks in the grain of the metal? Sometimes it may only crack a few grains of the material, which will not be seen, but may later start a crack in that area due to the other grains having more stress put on them.

The last specification is hardness. How hard is the material? This is measured on the Rockwell scale. Most low carbon steels start around a Rockwell hardness of B50 while 4130 will be around B90. The higher the number, the harder the material. After 100 on the B scale, it then goes to the Rockwell C scale, which means it is even harder. The Rockwell C scale starts at 20 which again is slightly harder the Rockwell B100. The Rockwell C scale also does the same, as number goes higher, the material is harder.

So now let me start talking about different materials that are the most common to have in your shop.

In the early 1940's the Society of Automotive Engineers (S.A.E.) or the American Iron and Steel Institute (A.I.S.I.) developed a numerical/alphabetical system to aid designers and engineers information on the many types of steel. This system for the S.A.E. and A.I.S.I has 4 to 5 characters to distinguish between these types of steels.

The first number is which family of steels it is derived from.

#1 means carbon steel 1xxx such as in the steel 1018

#4 means molybdenum steel such as 4130

#5 means chromium steel such as 5160

#8 means nickel chromium molybdenum steel such as 8620

The second digit indicates an added element.

The last 2 digits indicate the nominal carbon content of the steel. In 1018 this indicates a nominal carbon content of .18%. In 4130 this would indicate nominal carbon content as .30%.

These steels listed below are the most common for your shop use. There are many others but these are some of the most common to obtain from a steel supply company.

1018

A general purpose low carbon steel. It has good weld-ability and good machine-ability. It is available at most any steel company. It is easily shaped and formed steel.
Properties
Tensile Strength, psi 63,800
Yield Strength, psi 53,700
Elongation 15%
Rockwell Hardness B71

Hot rolled A-36 Angle and Flat stock

This has weld-ability but not as good as 1018 when you TIG weld it. It is easily shaped. Hot rolled will have a rougher appearance and measurement tolerances are not as tight as cold rolled 1018. Strength when compared to 1018 is less.

Continued pg. 94

Color Chart

STEEL AND STOCK CAR ALUMINUM, INC.

Tubing	Cr Round Bars
.028" Wall – Teal	4130 – Pink
.035" Wall – Black	1018 – Red
.049" Wall – Blue	12l14 – White
.058" Wall – Pink	1144 – Green
.065" Wall – Red	ETD150 - Teal
.065"+ Wall - Teal	
.083" Wall –	Aluminum Rounds
.095" Wall – Green	2024 – Gold
.120" Wall – White	7075 – Black
.156" Wall – Red	
.1875" Wall – Gold	Hr Flats & angles
.25" Wall – Blue	1/8" – White
	3/16 – Gold
	1/4" - Blue

A chart like this can be a very handy thing to have when you're shopping for stock in a big warehouse.

Cold and hot rolled flat stock - cold on the left and hot on the right.

Properties
Tensile Strength, psi 58,000
Yield Strength, psi 36,300
Elongation 20%

1020

This is the material that DOM tubing (less than 2 inch Diameter) is made from. It has good weld-ability and good machine-ability.
Properties
Tensile Strength, psi 87,000
Yield Strength, psi 72,000
Elongation 10%
Rockwell Hardness B89

4130

Also called cromoly, chrome-moly, cro-moly, but the proper name is Chromium Molybdenum. It has great strength, good weld-ability and good machine-ability. Be sure when purchasing 4130 it is stamped "COND N". This condition determines that the tubing was NORMAL-IZED. The heat treatment is stress relieving for the tubing, removing residual stresses created while forming the tubing. This results in a higher fatigue life and also has a big difference between the yield strength and the tensile strength. The elongation percentage is quite good also.

Continued pg. 95

In addition to tubing, it's nice to have at least a small stock of flat and angle stock.

Properties
   Normalized Tensile Strength 97,200
   Normalized Yield Strength 63,100
   Normalized Elongation 25.50%
   Normalized Rockwell Hardness B92

As you can see there are big differences between all the steels. There are so many more different types, but not necessarily for your shop, many are not needed or readily available. In most cases 1018 will be a good choice due to its characteristics and lower price. The hot rolled A36 is less expensive and makes great material for building your work and welding benches, and other fixtures in the shop.

1020 DOM and 4130 tubing work well for frame tubing. The only thing I would like to say is if your TIG welding ability is not that good or you are a VERY slow welder the HAZ (heat affected zone) is more forgiving with DOM. If you are a good TIG welder, then 4130 makes an excellent choice due to the increased strength, big difference between the ultimate tensile and the yield strength and the high elongation. DO NOT USE a Cromoly welding rod with 4130. The Cromoly rod builds high stress in the HAZ area and will need to be normalized. Use ER70-S rods. This ER70-S rod does NOT require any normalization unless the material is over .250 inch.

Be sure when you purchase your material it does have the data stamped on it. This data will tell you which mill it came from, what country is was made in, the size and thickness. It will have a Mil Spec number and batch number on it, if needed the steel company will have exact specifications numbers available for that material.

Of course, I always prefer the material I purchase to be made in the USA. But, how do I know

A company like Stock Car will have a bewildering array of material choices.

Round tubing is available in nearly every conceivable diameter and a big array of possible wall thickness.

Though the streamline tubing on the right might look sexy in certain situations, plain old round tube is generally stronger.

where to purchase these materials and what if I have questions? I use Stock Car Steel and Aluminum. They have quality products and good prices.

Have you ever noticed that on steel tubing, flat and angle, that one end has paint on it? What does the color of the paint determine? It easily distinguishes the different wall thicknesses in tubing and how thick the flat and angle is. The paint on the cold rolled bars makes it easy to see what material the bar is made from.

Tubing that has a thick, heavy wall also makes it easy to make your bushings and spacers on different projects. This can be either the 1020 DOM or 4130 tubing. Keeping small lengths of this thick wall tubing in different O.D. and wall thicknesses is a quick way to get your spacer job done!

Last of the materials I want to tell you about is aluminum and the different alloys it comes in.

6061-T6

This is one of the most common aluminums that you can buy. It has good machine-ability and good weld-ability. What does the T6 mean on the end of 6061? It means it has been heat treated (temper) and aged to give it a much higher strength. Where the problem comes about is when someone welds 6061-T6. In that area the material now goes back to 6061-T0, which is much softer and not as

Continued pg. 97

strong in this annealed condition. In order to bring it back to T6 you will need to send it to a commercial heat-treater to get it back to the higher strength T6 temper. This chart shows the differences between 6061-T6 and 6061-T0.

Properties

	6061-T6	6061-T0
Tensile Strength, psi	43,000	18,000
Yield Strength, psi	38,000	10,000

As you can easily see, if you weld 6061-T6 and it is a high strength carrying component, you will need to send it out and have it heat treated to bring the temper back to T6. You cannot do this correctly at your shop.

7075-T6

This is a higher strength of aluminum. Weld-ability and machine-ability are good. It does have the same problem that if it is welded, it will go back to a T0 state of temper. Again, if this is a high stressed part, send it out and get it professionally heat treated to bring the temper back to T6!

Properties

Tensile Strength, psi 65,000

Yield Strength, psi 58,000

2024-T351

This is a strong strength to weight ratio aluminum which has good machine-ability. It is NOT recommended to be welded together because it easily will become corroded after welding.

Properties

Tensile Strength, psi 68,000

Yield Strength, psi 47,000

3003 aluminum

This aluminum sheet is not heat treatable. It has excellent corrosion resistance, good formability and weld-ability. It can be easily bent and shaped.

Properties

Tensile Strength, psi 22,000

Yield Strength, psi 21,000

As you can now see, there are many choices for the home shop. If you have a special need, contact a company that specializes in metal sales. So much of the info I have found on some of the forums is totally not correct. I want to say a HUGE THANKS to the guys at Stock Car Steel and Aluminum. They let me go through their warehouse to take many photos and help to gather all the specifications for all the different materials. Check out their website for the materials and sizes for what you may need. www.stockcarsteel.com

Other suppliers are:
McMaster-Carr www.mcmaster.com
Airparts Inc. www.airpartsinc.com

There's a lot of information stamped on each piece of quality steel or aluminum, including the country of manufacture, as well as the OD and wall thickness (in the case of tubing).

All copy and images: Steve "Brewdude" Garn

Chapter Eight

Motorcycle Frame Jig

Is Your Motorcycle Frame Jig Aligned and Straight?

You get to a certain point in your progression on working and building your own motorcycles that you decide to build a frame, or just do a conversion. Maybe converting it to a hard-tail or changing the neck rake. There are plans and pictures of so many jig designs out there on the internet that people wonder, what design is best? This answer is easy and hard in the reasoning of my answer.

The hard answer is, what about a jig design?

There are so many designs and articles on frame jigs in books and on the internet, it really depends on a few things. How much area do you have for a frame jig? Will the frame jig need to be moved around? How much money you want to spend? And finally, what type of frame you want to build? A small displacement Café racer versus an extreme raked out fat tire frame is a big difference in the design you will want to use. Choose a design that will work for your needs and budget.

Pic 1. At the top of your tool list you will need levels and more levels: Short, long and digital.

The easy answer is? A straight jig! Yes, believe it, most jigs have some part of them that is not straight or square.

This article is intended to be sure that when you build or buy a frame jig it is straight! I have seen so many motorcycle frames over the many years (started my first shop in 1974) that have been sent in to either get a conversion done, or to be sandblasted and powder coated, that are not straight. Some of these frames had been converted or repaired in some way. Some are off almost new bikes that were never involved in any accident. So many people who build their own jigs use an existing frame thinking it is straight, but it may be crooked in many areas.

Pic 2. Next on the tool list, a speed square and some protractors.

I still have not found a factory frame that is straight, as measured on my jig and to my tolerances.

Pic 3. Don't forget the most basic of tools, a number of good metal rules.

Just one area that is not straight can throw the complete frame off. What do I mean by being crooked? The centerline of a frame should be straight from your front tire to your rear tire. The chain line from your front sprocket to the rear sprocket should be straight. It is easy to check the chain line. Look at the chain from the rear of the bike, the chain should be straight with no curve or twists. The neck tube, the frame backbone, the engine mounts should all be level and square to each other. The rear axle plates being squared up and level, all determine how straight the rear of the frame is. I still have not found a factory frame that is straight, as measured on my jig and to my tolerances. No matter what make or model don't assume the frame is lined up and straight.

So, let me tell you what you need and how to determine if the frame jig you are using is ready for you to build a straight frame. Even if the frame

Pic 4. A couple of plumb bobs are essential to your tool kit.

Pic 5. No matter what style they are, be sure to calibrate your levels.

Pic 6&7. You need to check your jig table along its length, then turn the level 90 degrees and check it again along its width.

Pic 8. It's essential that the neck upright is perfectly level.

jig is out of alignment you can determine what you will need to get it back in line once you determine where the problem is. It is much easier to understand what I am writing if you look at the photos as you read along.

It is important to have a selection of different levels as in (pic 1). You will need levels from 9 inch up to 48 inch. The 9 inch levels I prefer have a magnetic base. That way the magnet will hold it in place on a tube or support to check how level it is while doing other things on the frame. To be more accurate the digital levels are accurate within one tenth of a degree. The digital levels will determine what angle in degrees which is important for neck tube angle and other frame tubes. Hang your levels in a safe place so they won't get damaged or knocked out of calibration.

An assortment of squares and protractors (pic 2) help with your jig setup and can be used to determine how much angle you need when you bend tubes to build your frame. You can hold them up to the frame and adjust them until you get the look you want and then read the protractor to determine the angle in degrees of the bend. The rafter angle square, also known as a speed square, makes jig setup much easier and you will need two of these. Don't buy the plastic types because they have a tendency to warp and are as accurate. Just like the levels find a place to hang them so they won't be damaged.

For measuring the frame and setting up the jig you will need a few metal rules (pic 3). You will need these in different lengths so as you build your frame they can fit into different areas. I have small sizes of 6 inch and up to 48 inch. The one size I use the most is the 24 inch (61 cm). For longer lengths I use a tape rule. It is important to have some rules that not only read measurements in English, but also metric. This way no matter what brand of motorcycle frame you are working on you can use the proper measurement. Over the years I now use the metric measurements more often that the English.

Plumb Bobs (pic 4) are needed for the neck tube rod to be sure it is in proper alignment as you check or build your jig. Using plumb bobs to be sure that the backbone and rear triangle of the frame are aligned on the jig and with the other parts of the frame is an important step to a properly aligned frame. I actually have three plumb bobs and this way can keep one or two positioned in different areas of the frame so I can keep the frame level and in check as I work.

The first thing you need to do to be sure your frame jig is level and straight is to be sure your levels are, level! I was talking to a guy last week that bought an old house. He commented how every window and door in the house was out of plumb (not level or square). When he cleaned out an old shed behind the house, he found the previous owners tools. He found a 4' level in there and when he held it up to an existing doorway it showed level. The level was not calibrated to being level. With the new digital levels I calibrate mine before every build (pic 5). Just follow the directions that came with the digital level. The bubble levels can be adjusted. Loosen the screws that hold the level. Place the level on a table that is level. Adjust the level until the bubble shows level, the turn the level left to right and the bubbles should be exactly in the lines to show that it is still level. Don't assume that the levels at the stores are accurate. They could have been dropped or damaged. Check them out at the store before you buy them.

Remember,
jig centerline
is where alignment
begins.

Check your frame jig to be sure it is level both in length (pic 6) and in width (pic 7). With the jig being perfectly level in both directions you can set up the jig easily being sure it is plumb. When you set up the jig or checking an existing frame

Pic 9. As shown, the neck rod support needs to be level to the upright tube.

Pic 10. With the neck rod horizontal, place a plumb bob on the very end...

Pic 11. ...the plumb bob should point exactly to the centerline

Pic 12. Next, move the plump bob on the neck support rod next to the neck upright.

Pic 13. Place your speed square end up to centerline.

Pic 14. The axle plate center should line up with the speed square.

Pic 15. Here I square the axle plate jig to the centerline.

for being straight you can get accurate measurements. Once you know that the jig is truly level, the plumb bobs become very useful tools for checking that the backbone is centered in the frame. Unless it's level in all directions you really have no accurate reference point.The neck upright needs to be perfectly square with the table. If the neck upright is off it means that when you build a frame the neck will be off. The easiest way to check is by using your electronic level to see if it is 90 degrees off the jig table (pic 8). After checking the upright be sure that the neck rod that holds the neck cups is in alignment with the neck upright. What you need to do is move the neck rod straight up and check that it is level (pic 9). This is step 1 in alignment checking of the neck rod. The next step is now lowering the rod to level. Placing the plumb bob at the end of the support rod it should point exactly to the jig centerline (pic 10). The plumb bob should have the point exactly over the centerline of your jig (pic 11). Any slight deviation will place the neck tube at a side angle which is not what you want, not even if it's only off the slightest amount. Then move the plumb bob, still looped over the neck support rod, next to the neck upright (pic 12) and be sure that it is pointing exactly over the jig centerline. Since we are now sure the neck support rod is level in vertical and horizontal positions, you can move it to any angle and still retain alignment with the jig's centerline.

Now we will be sure that the axle plate holder is centered on the jig table. Placing the speed square so the edge is on the centerline is the first step (pic 13). Then check that your scribe line on the axle plate fixture has the mark on the centerline (pic 14). To be sure that the axle plate jig is square with the centerline use 2 speed squares as in pic 15. This assures that this fixture now is centered and square with the centerline.

This is when you can adjust your axle plate jig for the width between the 2 plates (pic 16). Some bikes will have one side offset more than the other, but be sure that you go off the centerline of the jig table. Remember, jig centerline is where alignment begins. Adjust the axle center bolt off the table for your frame ground clearance needed.

Pic 16. Now, adjust the axle plate jig for proper width.

Pic 17. And place the level on the axle plate support rod to be sure it is level

Pic 18. Be sure to double check all measurements.

103

Pic 19. Use a plumb bob on the rear of the frame to be sure it is over the jig centerline.

Pic 20. Use another plumb bob to check the backbone alignment.

Pic 21. The plumb bob should point to the jig centerline if the frame is straight.

Then place the digital level on the axle cross bolt (pic 17) to be sure it is level with the frame jig table. Be sure to double check your measurements and the level and square-ness as you go. In my opinion there is no such thing as checking measurements, level-ness, or square-ness too many times.

Now that you have checked your jig for proper alignment, you can be assured the frame you are building will be aligned also!

If you are modifying or checking a frame for straightness, this is now the time to place the existing motorcycle frame on the jig. After placing the neck of the frame on the neck support rod you will need to be sure the frame is positioned over the centerline. Many times if the frame is not straight you will notice that nothing else will measure level. Place a plumb bob at the rearmost section of the frame and place over the centerline (pic 19). Then measure the axle plates off the centerline on the jig table to see if the rear of the frame is straight. In pic 20 I am centering the plumb bob cord on the center of the backbone seeing how it lines up with the jig centerline. It should be over the centerline as in pic 21.

Checking the engine mounts to be sure they are level is an easy task. Just place an engine mount bolt in the jig and use the digital level as in pic 22. If the neck tube has a twist and is out of alignment many times this bolt will not be level!

Now that the frame is centered, level and square with the jig table you can check to see what the neck angle really is. Just hold your digital level on the neck rod (pic 23) and this will show the current angle of the neck tube. Now that you have checked your jig for proper alignment, you can be assured the frame you are building will be aligned also! (pic 24).

Pic 22. Place an engine mount bolt in the frame and check to see if it is level.

Pic 23. Final check to determine the neck angle.

Pic 24. At this point, the frame jig is aligned, and the frame itself is checked for straightness. Time to start chopping!

All copy and images: Steve "Brewdude" Garn

Chapter Nine

How to Cut & Miter Tubing

An Essential Part of Building a Custom Motorcycle

One of the first skills you will need to learn as you start to fabricate motorcycle frames is how to cut your tubing, and then miter it. A miter is simply the fitting of the end of one tube where it meets another tube. This fit is either on the end or in the middle of the other tube. The tube not mitered is referred as the parent tube. Some refer to mitering as notching the tube. Because I am writing this to someone who is

working at their home shop or maybe expanding their motorcycle shop skills, I will keep these demonstrations affordable. Many people think you need milling machines or expensive notchers to miter, but this is not true. I myself have two Bridgeport milling machines and only use them for mitering if I am producing many of the same items. Otherwise, I am much faster and get a tight miter working by hand, rather

It's not rocket science, but learning to fit tubing is a skill you're going to need if you intend to build custom motorcycles.

than using the milling machines.

The first thing you need to do is find a good supplier of grinding/sanding supplies to get the job done. Most times when you buy supplies at swap meets or yard sales the quality is bad and the item will wear out quickly or not do the job. The same is true from some of those tool discount stores that offer cheap foreign supplies. If it has a name brand you recognize or is made in the USA, you should be fine.

Recently I bought some cutting wheels and flap discs from some swap meets and then some from discount stores to see if the quality was as bad as it has been in the past. The cutting wheels that are USA made held up great and cut quickly and lasted, no matter where I bought them. The no-name oversea brands of cutting wheels actually came apart while cutting, and if they didn't, they lasted less than half the time that the USA made ones did. A cutting wheel that comes apart can hurt you or damage what you are working on. Buy quality!

What is a flap disc? A flap disc is made from overlapping strips of cloth sanding strips usually bonded to a fiberglass backing plate. It does a great job of grinding and blending. The various flap disc brands I bought for testing, whether from the swap meets or a good supply store looked pretty identical until I used them! The ones made in the USA, after being used for a while wore evenly and lasted a long time. The ones from overseas with no brand name, even though they looked identical, had slower cutting, and wore very unevenly, and were useless after a couple of uses.

Cutting wheels come in many sizes and thicknesses. For my die grinder I keep 2 inch and 3 inch in stock. The thickness I prefer is .045 inch. Anything thicker means it takes longer to cut, and the thinner ones seem to distort more when doing an angle cut. The wheels I use on my side grinder are 4 inches in diameter and .045 inches in thickness. Not only do you need to know the diameter and thickness of the cutting wheel, but you also need to know

Be aware, cutting wheels come in many diameters and thicknesses - and arbor diameters.

Sanding belts are available in many different grits.

A very handy tool, flap discs are made from overlapping pieces of cloth sanding strips.

As noted in the text, flap discs are available in two different styles, angle and flat.

A metal chop saw is a great tool to have in the shop - fast and easy.

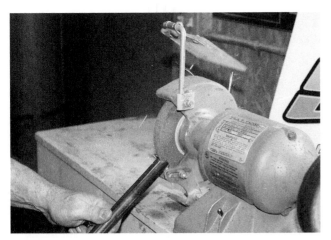

A bench grinder can be a great tool for shaping smaller diameter tubes.

the arbor size. The arbor is the shaft or screw that holds the wheel to your tool. There are many different diameters of arbors and you will need to know what size arbor hole wheel you need to order.

The same information is needed for flap discs. You will need to order the diameter and arbor hole for your side grinder. But, you have two more options when you order flap discs that you will need to know. You will have the option of different grits, from 36 grit, which is very course, to a flap disc of a grit of 120, which is a fine grit. I suggest trying a 60 or 80 grit flap disc to start with. The last thing to decide on when ordering your flap disc is the style. The styles available are an angle or a flat disc. Look at the pic on the left to understand the difference between the two. The one that I like to use the most is the angle style. It works well for mitering and also when you are trying to grind or blend some areas of metal together.

There are several ways to cut your tubing. The one way is to use a hacksaw to cut your tubing. This is the most economical way, but takes the longest and is very physical. The portable band-saw is a great tool to have. It cuts tubing straight or on an angle and can be used to cut tubes easily on an existing frame that you may be modifying. They are not cheap, but if you buy a name brand it will last you many years. The price will be around $300.

Another method is a metal chop saw. The metal chop makes cutting tubing fast and is capable of doing cuts straight but also on an angle. Cutting tubing on an angle makes it much faster to miter tubing that is on an angle. There are several makes and kinds out there. Some use an abrasive type cutoff wheel and others use a metal cutoff saw. The metal cutoff wheels are nice but you will need to pay more for one and be sure you get a name brand. The metal cutoff saws are different between the abrasive cutoff wheel and the metal cutoff wheel. Most steel blades have a maximum rpm of 2000 while an abrasive cutoff wheel has a maximum rpm of 4500 rpm. The metal cutoff saw I have has a rpm of 4000 rpm so you can easily see it will exceed the metal type cutoff wheel. Please check as different manufactures of the saws and wheels have different specifications. Again, buy a brand name saw.

The last method of cutting tubing is with a die grinder or your side grinder. I use the cutting wheels as I explained above. The die grinder is great for getting into tight areas especially cutting tubing and brackets off an existing frame. The side grinder works much faster but you need to pay attention or the side grinder can get away from you.

No matter what type of tool you decide to use, be sure to wear safety glasses. The safety shield is an extra piece of safety gear which gives you better protection if you also wear your safety glasses underneath them. It is easy for a stray piece of steel or material to go underneath the hood so that is why I suggest wearing safety glasses under the shield.

The other safety aspect is the fact that all the tools make noise! Some, more than others, it's a good idea to wear some type of noise protection for your hearing. See what feels the most comfortable for you to wear and will give you protection that will lower the sound to your ears.

For a cut that you want straight an easy way to get a guide is with 2 inch tape. Just cut off a piece long enough that it will overlap itself. Be sure the tape lays flat and that it lines up to itself. Then just cut along the edge.

For measurement marks on the tubing I use a sharpie. The line is fine enough and can easily be seen. If you mark it exactly and want to be sure you don't cut it too short, make a mark on which side you want to cut on. It is better to be a little long than a little short.

For small diameter tubing or larger tubing that is thinner, the bench grinder works great to grind your miters. I dress the grinding wheel down to a rounded edge versus the squared edge it comes with. After some practice you will be amazed how fast and how tight the fit can be.

After grinding, a small bench mounted belt

A small belt sander is a great tool for removing burrs on the outside of the tube.

Be sure to check the fit frequently as you cut your miter.

Use a speed square to check for a 90 degree miter.

109

A hacksaw will work, but a portaband is much easier.

You can also use cutting wheels with a die grinder or a side grinder.

A nice simple trick, use 2 inch tape to wrap the tube - and guide you for a straight cut.

sander removes the burrs and leaves a nice finished edge. Belt sanders come in many sizes, not only on belt length but also belt width. A good supplier of cutting supplies will have numerous belt grits available and different abrasive media in the same size length and width belt. I use 80 grit aluminum oxide belts for the 1x30 inch sanders. In my shop there are two 6x48 inch belt sanders. I keep 80 grit and 120 grit in stock. Remember, the lower the grit number the more course and fast the cutting it is. Many times you want a finer finish and that is when I use the 120 grit belts.

As you grind the tubing on the bench grinder you need to check it often to see how tight the miter fit is. When it gets close to a tight fit you also need to check out how square it is to the tube it is joining to. The speed square is a great tool to check this. Be sure to use the flat, wide base on the long tube and check how the alignment is. Then grind the side which needs to go down. Then, clean up the mitered edge on the belt sander.

For larger tubing, an angled flap disc on the side grinder is one method. Take your time and shape till the miter is a good fit. If you have trouble seeing what the shape should be there are several tube mitering software programs on the internet. It is easy to use these programs and in a few minutes will have a miter cut pattern printed out. You need to enter data for the diameter of the tube you will cut the miter on and the wall thickness of this tube. Then enter the data for the tube (parent tube) it will be welded to. You enter the O.D. (outside diameter) and the angle it will be attached. If the tube joins with the centerline of the tubes aligned, then the offset will be zero inches. If the tubing will join with an offset from each other, just enter the offset in inches. Next, you will print your pattern and then get scissors and carefully cut it out. Using scotch tape you then tape it to the tube you will grind the miter on. Be sure that the pattern aligns up to itself on the ends to assure a proper miter.

More options, a side grinder with a flap disc can be used to miter tubes.

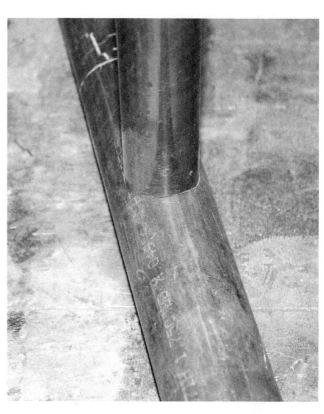

Here you can see the fit I created with the flap disc.

A small drum sander on a die grinder or drill is a good way to remove burrs on the inside of the tube.

If the miter is at an angle, start with an angle cut on the tube.

For cutting angle miters the flap wheel is the tool I use the most.

Again, grind slowly and check the fit often. It is easy to get too aggressive and over-grind an area.

When the fit gets close...

Always be sure to clean out the burrs on the inside of the tube you just mitered. A round file works fine. A small drum sander mounted on a die grinder or portable drill is faster and makes a nice smooth I.D. (inside diameter) of the tube. The I.D. de-burring is very important so that when you weld the miter, there will be no contamination from the burrs.

If the miter is not one that is 90 degrees it is time saving to do the initial cut at an angle. The side grinder with the flap disc works well to miter an angled one. The nice thing is, as you get more proficient with the flap disc on the side grinder you can miter tubes on an existing frame that needs mitering done. Again, check often as you start to grind the miter. When the fit gets close be sure to clean the I.D. since maybe some burrs are holding it out away from a tight fit miter. The fit needs to be tight.

To check the angle of the miter you need to use an adjustable protractor. Simply hold it to the parent tube and the other end on the mitered tube. There is a scale on the protractor and read what angle you have. If you need to adjust the angle, only grind a little at a time from one area and keep checking the angle. I have seen people get too aggressive and grind too much, and then have to keep going back and forth getting too much angle, then too little angle. Take your time.

On one of my 6x48 inch table belt sanders I have a 12 inch disc. The disc I use has a grit of 50 and removes material very fast. Just grind one side and then flip it to the side and grind that side. Check fit often and when you get close de-burr with the drum sander. This method works well with larger diameter tubing for 90 degree miters as well as angled miters. You can finish if needed with the flap disc on your side grinder for a tighter fit.

There are many methods to cut and miter tubing for your projects. Try different methods and use the one you find the most comfortable way to get the job done.

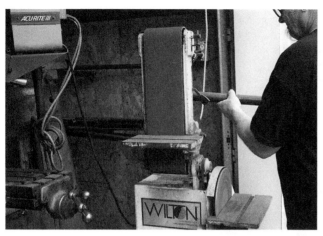

...use the sander to clean up burrs and smooth out the edges...

Check the angle of your miter with an adjustable protractor.

...the drum sander will help get the miter even tighter.

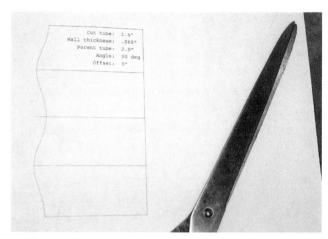

Tube mitering software prints out a pattern as shown.

This is what you want, a nice tight final fit.

Start by cutting the pattern out...

...tape the pattern on the tube...

...now just grind out the recessed areas.

You can use a disc sander as shown for mitering.

Photos and text by Steve "Brewdude" Garn

Q&A: Steve "Brewdude" Garn

Steve, give us a little background on you, how did you learn your technical skills, the welding and fabricating in particular?

When I was 15 years old I wanted to race motorcycles, I was already working on them but I didn't have the money to go out and buy race parts. So I built my own engines, and did my own suspension work. I learned to do my own frame mods when I was 17. That's where it all started. In 1974 I opened my first shop, we did porting work and some suspension work. I started building BMX bicycle frames to help pay for my motorcycle racing.

Can you run through the various projects you tackle in your current shop?

We do frame modifications, engine builds, suspension work, exhaust work, wiring and paint. I learned to paint out of necessity. People who buy a high-end bicycle frame often want a nice paint job and it is such a hassle to ship the frames to someone else and then there's always damage. We also build some bicycle components, like extremely light brakes for road bikes.

What kind of cautions do you give to anyone who wants to make or modify a motorcycle

frame? In terms of safety or unintended consequences of what they do.

It's unbelievable the frames that people bring in here. The welds are porous and weak. Then they grind off most of the bead - a lot of the strength is in that bead.

So, the first thing is, learn to weld. There are too many people who think they know it all, some of what they learned is just hearsay off the internet. Luckily, because of our high-end bicycle frames, I've learned a lot about tubing and the various alloys, and the best way to weld those tubes. When people start to weld, they need to start with something small. Something that, even if it does break, won't cause the bike to crash.

In reference to frames, does all the welding need to be TIG welding?

Those of us who TIG weld get snobbish. So I say yes. But all the Norton feather bed frames were made from Reynolds tubing that was brazed together. A lot of other English frames were manufactured that way too.

MIG welders should be adequate, but I've never seen anyone do what I consider a weld as nice as TIG with a MIG welder.

Any final words of wisdom to would-be chassis builders?

I encourage anyone to work on their own bike. But again, I started out with little things, like welding a bracket, not raking a frame and doing a hardtail conversion. I tell people to take small steps. And they need to keep an open mind. Even after 41 years I don't know everything. Welding technology changes and you have to keep up.

Chapter Ten

Oil Tank Fab

Custom Oil Bag How-To

Your oil tank is a very simple piece of any motorcycle build, one that is often overlooked and shoddily made. Poor mounting systems, inferior fittings, and the worst of all, improper plumbing placement, all can lead to one of the simplest pieces of your new bike being one of the most problematic. There are some very easy steps to follow that will assure your oil bag will always carry and supply sufficient lubrication for your engine, as well as stay intact and never fall apart from vibration.

Don't assume you have to buy an off-the-shelf oil tank for that new project in the garage. It turns out you can build your own from scratch or components with relative ease.

A FEW SIMPLE RULES
Capacity

A good guideline to follow for your motorbike's oil tank capacity is the three quart rule. Many old timers swear this is all you need, never an ounce more, never an ounce less. Others believe bigger engines, or baggers (that work harder and suffer from wind blocking bodywork) deserve more oil capacity. Three quarts is a good starting point. A stripped down chopper with a conservative engine and external oil filter, maybe even an oil cooler, can get away with a tad less than three quarts. It is best to consult with the manufacturer, engine builder, an experienced customizer, or all of the above if you intend to run less than three quarts. Keep in mind your oil filter may hold as much as ½ quart, depending on element size, and the oil cooler even more. This situation may allow you to run only 2 ½ quarts in your oil bag.

Mounting

We will get much deeper into this shortly, but a great rule of thumb is to always mount your oil tank with a minimum of three mounting points. A good thought to keep in your head is two mounts to counter gravity, one to counter vibration. In other words, two mounting points above or below supporting the weight of the tank, and one additional mount in any number of positions to quell vibration and the shifting mass inside your running motorcycle. Within reason, you cannot "over-mount" your oil tank, but transversely, you can "undermount" it. Additionally, in almost every case, some form of isolation is ideal. The most common form of isolation is rubber-mounting. There are many viable alternatives to rubber-mounting, such as polyurethane.

Common Fittings

It is best not to rush down to the hardware store and grab the coolest, most industrial looking fittings off the shelf, and head home to build your tank around these pieces. There is a great chance you could work yourself into a

All of the parts, or reasonable facsimiles, are available from your local steel yard or supply catalog. The bungs we use are fancier, but essentially the same as quality bungs you can find from any manufacturer.

Prior to tacking the ends together, check for proper alignment all the way around the circumference of the two pieces to be mated. If adjustments need to be made, now is the time.

Once alignment is assured, tack the cap and body together. It is a good idea to go from one side to another, and then front to back.

117

After you have tacked your first four spots, go around the tank and add additional tacks.

Flip the tank over and use the same technique to tack this end.

Now you can begin finish welding. It is a great idea to jump from one end of the tank to the other and alternate sides to minimize warpage while welding.

corner later down the road when you need to replace a fitting when you are miles from home, or you need a hard-to-find tap to repair damaged threads. Additionally, hardware stores can be chock full of inexpensive and inferior fittings that are intended to feed an icemaker, not withstand the rigors of your high horsepower wheelie machine. Buy quality fittings.

The size of your fittings is also very important. It is not recommended that your feed, return, or vent is smaller than 1/8 NPT. Any smaller and a bottleneck is created, and your engine could starve for oil, or a restricted return or vent could create numerous issues with gaskets and seals.

Proper Placement of Plumbing

If you are building your own oil tank, there is a great chance you are planning out the placement of your plumbing. You may want to run your vent or return lines on the top, the bottom, even the sides, front, or back. This is all fine if you assure that within the tank your vent and return outlet is above the full oil level. If not, you will surely see issues with your engine puking oil out upon every startup, and possibly while riding. Not the best scenario.

For the most part, your feed line should always be on the bottom. It just makes sense to let gravity do its work. If you absolutely need to run your feed line in a different location, make sure the interior inlet is close to the bottom of the tank. Additionally, you must prime your system prior to startup.

For our project, we are building and mounting a simple five inch round oil bag on a hardtailed Sportster chopper we are mocking up.

When you finish your last weld, it is a good idea to leave a small portion open, or to locate a pilot hole for a later bung hole. This prevents pressure inside the tank from blowing out the last bit of your weld.

You can begin to grind down the bulk of your weld now. It will be far easier to grind now than when your bungs and mounts are installed. You can use a hand grinder, or....

...if you're lucky enough to have a belt grinder, use that.

119

Cleanup you do now will save time in the future. Jay is using a 3 in DA to cleanup marks left from spinning the ends. Though barely noticeable they will be a nuisance for a polisher to remove later if the tank is plated.

Using witness marks to keep us centered, we identify where we want mounts to go. Don't locate your hole too far from the frame, as you want to leave enough material to shape your mount for a tight joint.

Now we are ready to mount the tank. We are using off-the-shelf rubber mounts that are intended for gas tank mounting.

After finding our mounting locations, we use a piece of angle iron to transfer the vertical measurement from one side to the other.

To start, we mark the center of the tank. To make alignment a bit easier, we laid down two witness marks so we can evenly space the tank relative to the seat post.

Use a center punch to firmly establish your location.

Then drill your pilot hole. Be sure to use a small enough drill for your pilot that your hole saw or rotobroach will not be sloppy when drilling.

We choose to use a rotobroach for drilling our mounting holes. A hole saw or even a traditional drill bit will work fine, if proper care is taken.

A quick test fit shows that our mounts are going to be in a great spot.

Upon tacking the mounts in place, it is a good idea to place a couple of long bolts into the threads to assure alignment. You can look from the long end of the tank and see if the bolts are both oriented correctly.

To be sure the mounts are on the same plane relative to the oil tank's centerline, you simply lay a straight edge across the two mounting surfaces.

With the mounts bolted to the tank, you can now mark your trim lines.

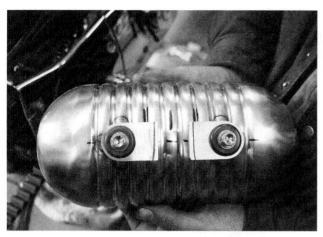

You will notice that with proper layout and meticulous locating of the mount holes, our trim lines are nearly identical.

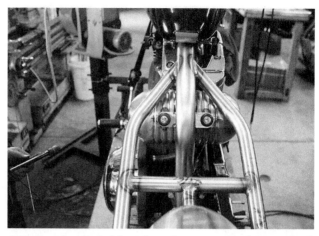

With each side held on by a few strong tacks, we check the fit. Be sure that there is no undue stress placed on the rubbermounts - eventually this will lead to failure. Your mounts and tank should line up perfectly.

Only a small amount of grinding is needed to achieve the right fit. Be sure to leave a nice bevel for your weld.

For our long, bottom mount, we are able to simply measure for the trim line, as we know we will be centering this mount on the seatpost and oil tank.

You may need an extra set of hands for this part of the mockup. After double and triple checking our alignment, our first tacks are set.

We are using an endmill the same size as the seatpost to notch the mount to an airtight fit.

The mount slips into place with a perfect fit. We did need to go back to the mill once to take out just a little more material. This tab gets a heavy bevel prior to welding. After the rest of the tank is finished and welded, we will add gussets to both sides of this mount to provide a little more support.

Now we will locate our fitting bungs. It is always ideal to locate your feed line on the opposite side from your drive belt or chain.

When locating your vent and return lines, it is a good idea to place them opposite your feed line. This will allow the returning oil to circulate before it is introduced right back into the system.

After fitting the filler hole, we need to trim the filler bung so it does not reach too far down into the tank, prohibiting the tank from being filled correctly.

After cleaning up the cut in the lathe, the filler bung is ready to be welded in.

All that is left now is pressure testing and coating. Keep in mind that while you may not be building this exact tank, the principles and techniques are universal.

Chapter Eleven

Bars from Scratch

Two sets of Bare Knuckle Bars

The look and feel of any custom motorcycle (or stocker, for that matter) can easily be changed by adding a new set of bars. A handlebar swap is one of the cheapest and quickest ways to customize your bike. But in the event that you cannot find something that fits your needs perfectly, you are left with three choices; settling for something close, commissioning a pair to be made, or making your own. Obviously we think making your own is the coolest way to solve this problem. We are going to show you how to do a couple different styles of bar. The same basic principles apply to most any style of bar, so take our groundwork and run with it.

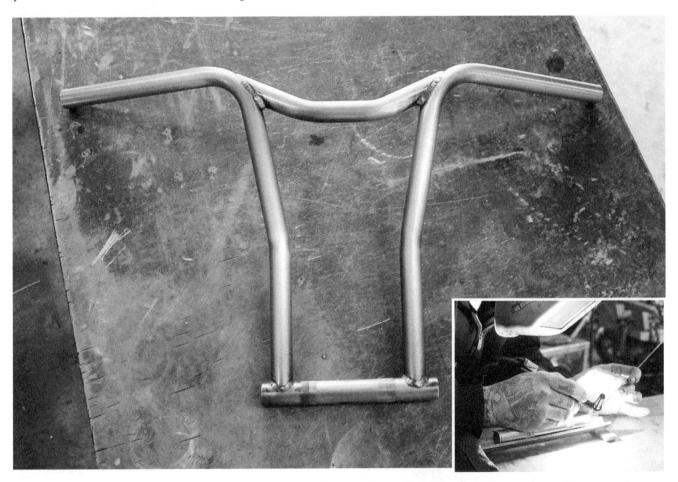

Narrower than most, this set of bars requires good welding skills, and was built with provisions for internal wiring and/or throttle.

To the right you will see the three basic options for one inch handlebar tubing. On the left you will see our stainless steel selection. You will notice that it is substantially larger in wall thickness, at .120 inch. In the middle you will see our D.O.M. example, in which you can see no seam, and the .095 inch wall thickness is a bit smaller than the stainless. The E.R.W. section on the right shares the same wall thickness as the D.O.M., but you will notice the presence of a seam on the bottom side of the I.D.

MATERIAL COMPOSITION AND WALL THICKNESS

The first decision to make when fabricating your own bars, is choosing a material. For all intents and purposes you are left with only two choices; stainless steel or mild steel tubing. Of course you could choose chromoly or some exotic material, but unless you just want to spend extra money or be able to say you did something, there is no reason to use anything but stainless or mild.

For bars that are to be chrome, nickel, or brass plated, powder coated or painted, you may be best instructed to choose mild steel for your bars. For our application, mild steel tubing comes in two forms; D.O.M., or Drawn Over Mandrel, and E.R.W., or Electric Resistance Weld. Oftentimes D.O.M. is referred to as "seamless", which it is not. D.O.M. is a welded tubing that is run through a mandrel during the forming process to normalize the weld seam, and as a result, the seam is essentially undetectable. It is not the lack of a detectable seam that makes D.O.M. desirable, rather the normalized weld. This process makes the tube a stronger product than it's E.R.W. counterpart. There is actual seamless tubing, cold drawn seamless, to be exact, but it is not very common, size options are limited, and it is very costly.

The industry standard for handlebars is E.R.W. There is nothing wrong with using E.R.W. for your bars, just so long as you pay special attention to the orientation of the weld seem when bending. You want the weld seam to be perpendicular to the centerline of your bends. In other words, the weld seam should never stretch or

As we have made these bars previously, we know the precut length. To start, Jay cuts the stock to length. If you are bending up a set you have not made before, you may want to leave a few extra inches. We are using .120 inch wall stainless steel for this set.

After cutting the bar stock to length, it is a great idea to deburr the ends. This will save your hands, and it will minimize wear on your bender.

127

One extra step we like to do is pre-polish the material prior to bending. This keeps the extra grit and grime out of your bender, and makes a more presentable piece after the work is done. We polish ours in the lathe using Scotchbrite. Do not perform function if not properly trained!

shrink. Doing so will increase your chances of fractures and cracks. The one other instance in which you should reconsider using E.R.W. is when fabricating mitered bars, or any bars that require cutting and welding. In such cases, it is desirable to use D.O.M.

You will find many wall thickness options when looking through both E.R.W. and D.O.M. selections. For the most part, .095 inch, or 13 gauge, is the ideal selection. Using .095 inch will keep your options open regarding internal throttles and other standardized accessories. .095 inch is also sufficiently strong for most any application.

If you are looking for a bar that can be polished and needs no further coating, look no farther than stainless steel. But alas, not all stainless steel is created equal. At most steel yards you will find both 304 and 316L. In nearly every instance the 316L will be more costly than 304. If you can afford it, buy the 316L; it has better rust resistance qualities. Most stainless steel tubing will be welded tubing, but there are some sources for "seamless" stainless steel tubing. Stainless steel seamless tubing is very nice, but would be considered by most overkill for handlebars, especially considering the cost increase.

After the material is properly prepared, we lay the bar stock on the table, and measure for the first bend. These bars are narrow, and we like them that way. So we are making each end of the bar 8 inches. This will allow for all of your controls, grip, etc, but there will be little extra room. You may want to start with 9 inch or 10 inches.

With stainless steel you may find your wall thickness choices limited. While most internal throttles require an outside diameter of 1.000 inch and a wall thickness of .095 inch, you will be hard-pressed to find a stainless steel tube of any sort that fits these requirements. Most steel yards will jump from .083 inch to .120 inch wall thickness. In this case it is best to err on the side of safety and opt for the .120 inch wall. This will be only slightly heavier, but much stronger. If you intend to run an internal throttle, you will need to plan ahead. It is a good idea to machine the throttle end to the proper I.D. prior to bending your bars. It can be near impossible to do so afterwards.

While one inch handlebars are by far the most common size for bars on custom motorcycles, there is also the call for larger diameter bars, such as 1 ¼ inch, and sometimes even larger, as well as 7/8 inch, commonly used on British and Japanese bikes. For the larger bars you may find yourself needing to step down in the riser area to use the more common one inch risers, and you will most likely need to step down again in the grip area. This is most easily accomplished using 1 ¼ inch .120 inch or .125 inch tubing so that you can slide right over the one inch section(s). For 7/8 inch bars you can run between .095 inch (13 gauge) and .120 inch (11 gauge). The same principles apply to these bars as with one inch bars, as discussed above.

These are the 2 most common shoes for our Mittler Brothers 180 degree bender, for 1 inch bars. Different shoes allows us to change the impact a particular bend has on the size, shape, and appearance of the bars.

You can see that the first mark has been lined up with the beginning of the bend area on the shoe. Jay's left hand is setting the digital readout to zero so we know that the indicated angle is true.

As Jay steps on the air-over-hydraulic control, his eyes are focused on the DRO, as opposed to the material.

While the bender is still engaged with the first bend, Jay fastens a digital level, and zeroes the readout. This will keep us honest with each bend, relative to the offsets each bend requires.

After the first bend is complete, and the digital level is secured, Jay removes the tube from the machine and places a mark indicating the termination of the first bend.

Measuring from the end of the first bend, a mark is applied where the second bend is set to start.

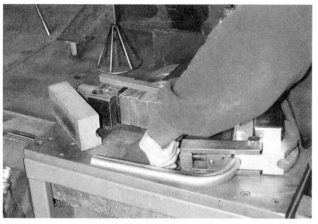

Notice the bender is 45 degrees through its stroke - to accommodate the downward offset of the handle area of the bar. We must start from this end, or there would not be enough adjustment to complete the bars.

Back at the table, the end of the previous bend is again identified, and the start point for the next is marked.

These bars call for a 35 degree offset. You can see how the handle area dips far down below the table of the bender, hence the beginning offset.

Since these are very narrow bars, we are only allowing 4 ½ inches between bends. This is a special request. Normally they are a bit wider to ensure fitment across a broad spectrum of applications.

At this point, the DRO is set to zero, and the bend can be completed.

As the third bend is finalized, note the digital level reads 34.8, as opposed to the initial 35 - which demonstrates the amount of twist that occurs when bending. This will be remedied on a flat bench later.

131

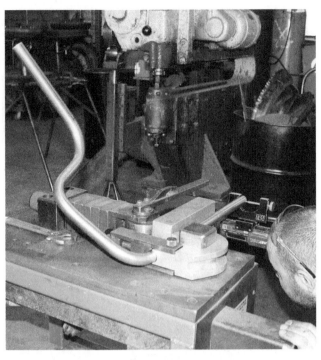

After carefully laying out the final bend, Jay meticulously adjusts the bars to their initial zero point.

Digital level will interfere with machine if not removed. Angle of bars gives an idea why we offset the bender in the 2nd and 3rd bends. Had we started from the other end, there would be no clearance for this final bend.

With a close eye on the DRO, the final bend is made.

Following the same formula throughout the entire sequence, the last bend point is identified.

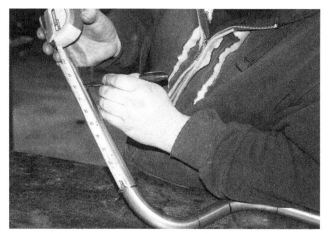

1) We knew the overall length of the bars when we started, but we left a little to be trimmed. Using the mark from the last bend, Jay marks the final cut.

2) This picture shows how many marks are made, and how time consuming bar fab can be.

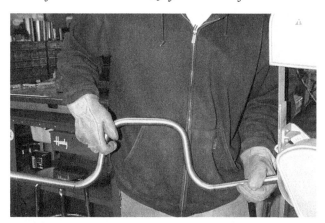

5) The outside edge of the cut is then deburred, this time on the belt grinder.

3/4) The extra few inches are trimmed off the end, making both sides identical. Inset: After being cut in the saw, the ends need to be deburred. This can be accomplished with a simple deburring tool, a rattail file, or a rotary burr.

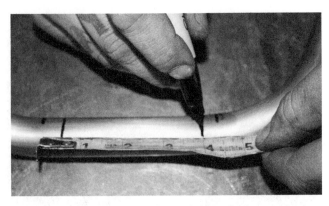

1) Using the old marks from the bends, layout for knurling is marked out. Bars will be used on risers centered 3 ½ inch apart. The knurl will be applied to each side of the 3 ½ inch marks.

2) The knurl is now applied to the outer edge of first mark. It takes a few trips around the tubing with increasing pressure to make the knurl deep enough.

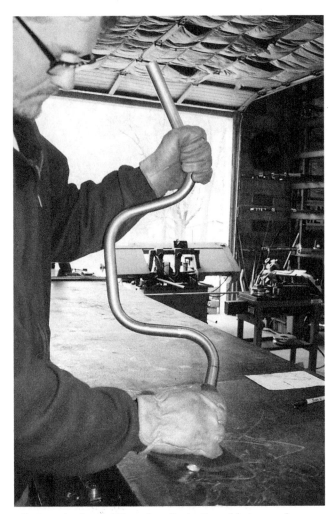

4) Finish them off with a little Scotchbrite and cleaner.

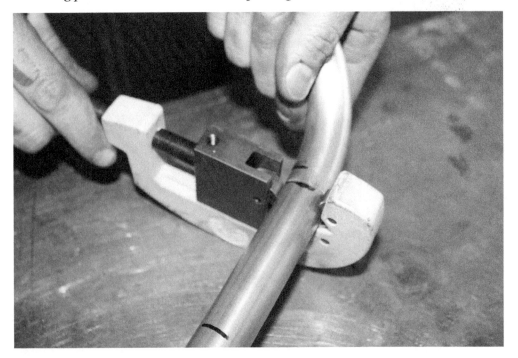

3) To make the knurl wide enough, a second knurl is applied to the inside of the mark. Make note of how tight the tool was on the first application, and duplicate that depth for the second side. This way the two will match.

Bar Fab #2

This set of bars is a bit more complicated, but shows you the basics of fabricating a set of bars that require cutting, notching, and welding. For this bar we will be using 1 inch .095 inch wall D.O.M. mild steel tubing.

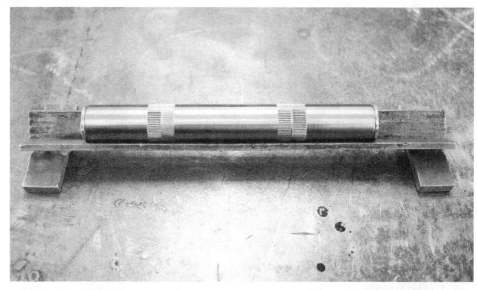

*Top right:
To start we knurled the center piece of the bar - much easier to do this now than later. Next we laid the bar in a piece of angle iron to keep the tubing from moving while the end caps are welded on.*

The end caps are tacked on. The center piece was cut to length and faced in the lathe prior to tacking, so we are sure that the ends will be perfectly square.

Using 1/16 inch filler rod, the entire end cap is welded to the center piece.

Using 1/16 inch filler rod, the entire end cap is welded to the center piece

Using a 3 inch dual action sander, or DA, the surface is blended, and the transition disappears.

There are numerous ways to polish your welds down. Here we chose to start with a heavy flap wheel. It's important to go very slow and be precise with the strokes - it's easy to cut too deep with this wheel.

Next step is to create a port for possible internal wire and/or cables. Layout fluid is applied, using a height gauge two lines are scribed. These measurements will allow for a 1 ¼ inch long oval to be cut in the...

Heaviest part of the weld has been removed with the flap wheel, this 2 inch medium conditioning disc will take the remainder of the weld down to the surface.

...bottom center of the bar. Instead of using this ½ inch roughing mill, you could drill two ½ inch holes to create the ends of your oval, and then use a hand file or die grinder to finish off the oval.

On the opposite side from the center slot, there needs to be two large holes to allow wires or cables to transfer from the upright of the bar to the center-piece. Knowing that we want the 1 inch uprights on 6 inch centers, we laid our center lines out in layout fluid again.

The first drill is actually a center drill. This will keep the pilot hole from drifting across the tubing.

After sizing up to a ¾ inch drill, we have large access ports in our center section. The key here is to go as large as possible, so the wire/cable has sufficient room to move through upon installation. The hole cannot be too large, however, as you must have enough room for a quality weld.

The layout fluid is removed and the holes deburred. This is the last attention this component needs prior to welding.

With each end coped, you will notice that the edges have been beveled for welding, as well as the offset that was applied when notched. This will give each side its respective pullback.

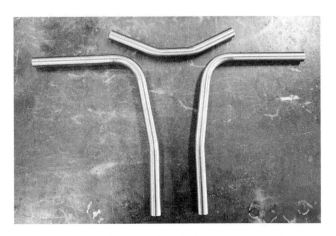

The same guidelines and techniques used on the first set of bars were used to bend up these three pieces. Now we need to mate them all together.

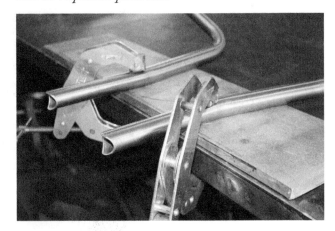

To tack the center piece to the two uprights, we are clamping the pieces to a flat aluminum plate. This will allow us to triple check all measurements and assure that the assembly is square.

Each side of the assembly is placed in the notcher with the handle area at its required offset. Using a 1 inch end mill, the notcher creates the perfect notch, or cope. (See Chapter 9 for notching options.)

The center piece is held up against the uprights and the center is found.

138

While holding the centerpiece tightly in position, the joints are tacked.

...fit much nicer with minimal hand work. While the notcher does make a beautiful and precise notch, there is still some cleanup left prior to welding.

After the initial tacks all measurements are checked and rechecked. For the time being, this is as far as the assembly will be welded.

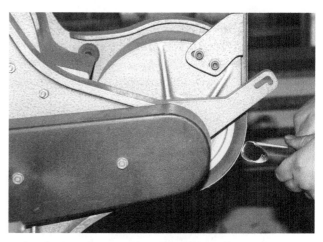

After both ends are notched and fitted, ends are cleaned up and beveled. This can be done with any number of grinders, but we again choose the belt grinder.

The center piece must be notched, correct angle is important. Note we are mating 1 inch to 1 inch tubing, size of end mill is 1 1/8 inch. This notch will contact the uprights in the top bend area. For this reason the added end mill size will make the notch...

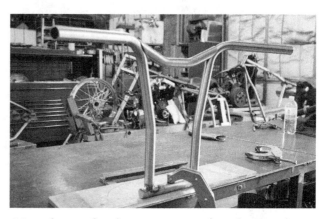

Now that perfect fitment is assured, tacking and final welding can begin. As always, tack and check, tack and check.

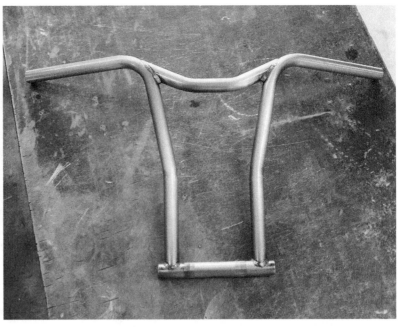

It is very important to constantly check your measurements and angles when welding outside of fixturing.

And if your patience holds out, you check and recheck your measurements, you will come up with a great looking set of handlebars.

Below: One more, totally different set of bars from BKC. These "flat tracker" style bars provide the rider with a broader grip and increased control, yet utilize all of the stock accessories. The powder coat matches the rest of the coating on the bike.

Above: Hardly a chopper, this 2012 Sportster was hardtailed and customized by Paul and Bare Knuckle Choppers. Many of the stock pieces were used or altered, creating a very cool, but budget friendly custom. Scott Takes of Underground Art Studios laid down the beautiful paint.

Q&A: Paul Wideman

How about a little background, how long have you been involved with motorcycles?

I've been involved with custom motorcycles since maybe 1999. I really wanted a custom bike, like my dad had when I was young, so I bought a 1957 Sportster with a custom frame and a few cool parts. I took it to my Dad's house and built a bench and bought a welder. I started making parts and frequenting a few bike shops, became friends with one of the owners and then started working there.

How did you come to own your shop, Bare Knuckle Choppers.

Around 2002 I built a frame jig. About this time I asked the owner of the shop for a full time job for the last time, and when he denied the request, I quit my day job and opened Bare Knuckle Choppers. Best decision I've ever made. but looking back, I had no idea what I was in for.

Tell us a little about BKC.

Bare Knuckle Choppers is a hands-on motorcycle shop. We produce high quality parts, both fabricated and machined, with a very strong focus on American manufacturing. We also build a few ground up customs each year, and modify a few existing bikes. We pride ourselves on craftsmanship and doing things the right way.

Where did you learn your fabrication skills?

In tech school during my high school years, in my garage, in a motorcycle shop, and through a whole lot of scrap and mistakes.

A person building a custom bike needs a variety of skills (besides a basic mechanical ability), among those skills, which is the most essential and first one a novice should learn?

LEARN HOW TO WELD!!! Too many guys go buy a TIG machine and start selling handlebars and sissybars. There is so much more to it than a "pretty rainbow" on stainless or "stacking dimes" on DOM tubing. What does your v-groove look like? How is your metal prepped? Are you using the correct rod? What does the underside of your weld look like? There is so much more to it than

what meets the eye. Literally.

In addition to hand tools, drills and such, which is the first piece of equipment a person should buy for a home-based or small shop?

A quality TIG machine and then a lathe. You cannot make quality motorcycles without those two essentials. Unless of course you or your customers have very deep pockets, and you can afford the time and labor involved with outsourcing welding and machining.

What are the mistakes that first time builders and fabricators make?

I would say a combination of biting off more than they can chew and failing to be humble. I've been at this professionally for 11 years now, and I really have a lot to learn. Doing research and asking questions is the key.

If you were to hire a person to work in the shop, what kind of skills and knowledge would you expect them to have?

Haha! Funny you ask. I am always looking for qualified TIG welders. It's tough to find a guy or girl who I can sit down and then watch them weld properly. Basic machining skills are a plus. If you have the drive and those skills, I can teach you the rest pretty quick.

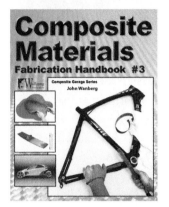

COMPOSITE MATERIALS - FABRICATION HANDBOOK #3

Composite Fabrication Handbook #3 continues this practical, hands-on series on composites with helpful how-to projects that cover a variety of topics geared toward assisting home-builders in completing their composite projects. Handbook #3 starts off where Handbook #2 ended, expanding on mold-making techniques including special methods for creating molds and composite copies of existing parts, fabricating molds from clay models, and mak-

ing advanced mold systems using computer modeling software. Several alternative methods of fabricating one-off parts are presented in this book, including molding over frameworks and human forms, as well as using stock composites to build simple structures.

This is the book for anyone who's ready to advance beyond the methods and projects presented in Handbooks #1 and #2.

| Nine Chapters | 144 Pages | $27.95 | Over 400 photos, 100% color |

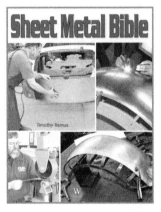

SHEET METAL BIBLE

Sheet Metal Bible is a collection of sheet metal fabrication projects, everything from simple shaping operations to multi-piece creations like fenders and motorcycle gas tanks. While some of the craftsmen seen in this book work with only hand tools, others prefer the English Wheel. The book is filled with work by legendary fabricators like Ron Covell, Rob Roehl and Bruce Terry.

Deciding how best to fabricate a particular part means deciding whether to shrink, stretch or simply bend the metal into the requited shape. Not to worry, each shaping method is covered in detail, so whether your project rolls on two wheels or four, needs parts make from aluminum or steel, is simple or complex, there is something in this new 176 page book to help you turn that dream into reality.

| Ten Chapters | 176 Pages | $29.95 | Over 350 photos, 100% color |

ADVANCED CUSTOM MOTORCYCLE WIRING REVISED

The one job that even the best mechanics avoid is wiring. Those worries are now over with help from the revised edition of Advanced Custom Motorcycle Wiring. This book uses Chapter One to cover the basics of DC Electricity and Chapter Two to explain Batteries, Starters and Alternators. Next up are the schematics and a discussion of factory harnesses, for both early and late-model Harley-Davidsons.

Jeff Zielinski, owner of NAMZ Custom Cycle Products and designer of all their wiring harnesses and components, is the author of this revised Motorcycle Wiring book. In addition to a discussion of factory Harley-Davidson Wiring harnesses, Jeff uses over half the book to describe the various harness options available to a person building a custom bike.

| Twelve Chapters | 144 Pages | $27.95 | Over 300 photos, 100% color |

CUSTOM BIKE BUILDING BASICS

Custom Bike Building Basics is the basic bible that at-home builders need to build and modify their own motorcycle.

But first you need a place to work and a set of tools to work with. Chapter One covers these topics and more, including the need for a quality compressor and a decent motorcycle lift. Basic skill building is next, starting with Steel Fabrication and Welding.

Grass roots bikes are often built using a "donor bike" as the foundation and source for the majority of parts.

This great book from Wolfgang Publications and Cycle Source Magazine, Custom Bike Building Basics is the one book you need before you tear into that donor bike and begin the process of creating your own motorcycle.

| Sixteen Chapters | 144 Pages | $24.95 | Over 450 photos, 100% color |

Wolfgang Publication Titles

For a current list visit our website at www.wolfpub.com

ILLUSTRATED HISTORY

Ultimate Triumph Collection	$49.95
American Police Motorcycles - Revised	$24.95

BIKER BASICS

Custom Motorcycle Fabrication	$24.95
Custom Bike Building Basics	$24.95
Custom Bike Building Advanced	$24.95
Sportster/Buell Engine Hop-Up Guide	$24.95
Sheet Metal Fabrication Basics	$24.95
How to Fix American T-Twin Motorcycles	$27.95

COMPOSITE GARAGE

Composite Materials Handbook #1	$27.95
Composite Materials Handbook #2	$27.95
Composite Materials Handbook #3	$27.95

HOT ROD BASICS

How to A/C Your Hot Rod	$24.95
So-Cal Speed Shop's How to Build Hot Rod Chassis	$24.95
Hot Rod Wiring	$27.95
How to Chop Tops	$24.95

CUSTOM BUILDER SERIES

How to Build A Café Racer	$27.95
Advanced Custom Motorcycle Wiring - Revised	$27.95
How to Build an Old Skool Bobber Sec Ed	$27.95
How To Build The Ultimate V-Twin Motorcycle	$24.95
Advanced Custom Motorcycle Assembly & Fabrication	$27.95
How to Build a Cheap Chopper	$27.95

MOTORCYCLE RESTORATION SERIES

Triumph Restoration - Unit 650cc	$29.95
Triumph MC Restoration Pre-Unit	$29.95

SHEET METAL

Advanced Sheet Metal Fabrication	$27.95
Ultimate Sheet Metal Fabrication	$24.95
Sheet Metal Bible	$29.95

AIR SKOOL SKILLS

Airbrush Bible	$29.95
How Airbrushes Work	$24.95

PAINT EXPERT

How To Airbrush, Pinstripe & Goldleaf	$27.95
Kosmoski's New Kustom Painting Secrets	$27.95
Pro Pinstripe Techniques	$27.95
Advanced Pinstripe Art	$27.95

TATTOO U Series

Advanced Tattoo Art - Revised	$27.95
Cultura Tattoo Sketchbook	$32.95
Tattoo Sketchbook by Jim Watson	$32.95
Tattoo Sketchbook by Nate Powers	$27.95
Into The Skin The Ultimate Tattoo Sourcebook (Includes companion DVD)	$34.95
American Tattoos	$27.95
Tattoo Bible Book One	$27.95
Tattoo Bible Book Two	$27.95
Tattoo Bible Book Three	$27.95
Tattoo Lettering Bible	$27.95

TRADE SCHOOL SERIES

Learning The English Wheel	$27.95

LIFESTYLE

Bean're — Motorcycle Nomad	$18.95
George The Painter	$18.95
The Colorful World of Tattoo Models	$34.95

GUIDE BOOKS

Honda Motorcycles - Enthusiast Guide	$27.95

Sources

Airparts Inc.
www.airpartsinc.com

Creative Metalworks
763-784-2997

Though known primarily as a four-wheel hot rod fabrication shop, there isn't much this duo can't tackle. From welding to machining to restoring old classics, Kurt and Pat simply get it done with skill and hard work in lieu of bright lights and fanfare.

Donnie Smith Custom Cycles
763-786-6002

It's hard to tell what you will find in Donnie's shop. Collectively the crew has way over a hundred years of experience. And though they're known as a custom bike shop, you never know what you're going to find when you walk through the door. On one hoist you might find a bone-stock Indian twin, and on the next, Cindy Crawford's late model custom Softail.

Bare Knuckle Choppers
Paul Wideman
636-338-4355

Another motorcycle nut, tech writer and shop owner, Paul is the power behind Bare Knuckle Choppers; the shop that builds not only complete bikes, but their own line of parts including frames, forks, oil tanks and much more. Whether it's a frame or a component, the parts they sell, and the parts they use in the builds, are of American origin.

Steve "Brewdude" Garn
828-406-6668
brewracingframes.com

A frequent contributor to Cycle Source and The Horse, Steve is also a total motorcycle nut, welder and fabricator. In between all this motorcycle work, Steve builds very high end bicycle frames, and holds occasional seminars for anyone who wants to learn how to build one of their own.

Shadley Bros.
781-447-4454
shadleybros.com

Shadley Bros. is actually one part of a larger operation. Paul and Mark have this ability to keep a lot of balls in the air at once. The juggling act includes AutoTec, an automotive repair shop with a separate body shop, a four-truck towing service, a mostly-Harley motorcycle repair and mild customizing shop, and a complete custom motorcycle fabrication shop.

Stock Car Steel and Aluminum
www.stockcarsteel.com

Mississippi Welders Supply
www.mwsco.com
507-474-2910

McMaster-Carr
www.mcmaster.com

CPSIA information can be obtained
at www.ICGtesting.com
Printed in the USA
FSOW03n0851021214
3661FS

9 781935 828792